P9-AQZ-097

Imperialism and the Corruption of Democracies

Herman Lebovics

IMPERIALISM AND THE CORRUPTION OF DEMOCRACIES

Duke University Press   Durham & London

2006

© 2006 Duke University Press

All rights reserved

Printed in the United States of America

on acid-free paper ∞

Designed by C. H. Westmoreland

Typeset in Adobe Caslon

by Keystone Typesetting, Inc.

Library of Congress
Cataloging-in-Publication Data
Lebovics, Herman.
Imperialism and the corruption of
democracies /
Herman Lebovics.
p. cm.
Includes bibliographical references and index.
ISBN 0-8223-3661-8 (cloth : alk. paper)
ISBN 0-8223-3697-9 (pbk. : alk. paper)
1. Imperialism. 2. Imperialism—History.
3. Democracy.
I. Title.
JC359.L324 2006
325′.32—dc22   2005027151

for Aldona

CONTENTS

When the white man turns tyrant,

it is his own freedom that he destroys.

—GEORGE ORWELL,

"Shooting an Elephant"

The opening quotation from the onetime officer of the Burmese colonial police announces this book's theme: colonies are dangerous to the health of democracy. They act as a sweet but poisoned pill to the states that have eagerly gulped them down. My essays on this theme were written for different occasions over more than a decade. When I sat down recently to reread them, I found a coherence to my various critical efforts. Each piece, I saw, added weight to an overarching concern with how imperial strivings harm the chances for an egalitarian social order. The frequent recurrence of this theme may have been my own colonial unconscious guiding me; but for sure, my conscious research has long been circling over this terrain.

In earlier work, I have found it fascinating to trace the general impact of conquest, rule, and exploitation on the countries that conquered colonial empires. The catalogue of these influences is impressive. The colonies have gifted Europe with economic subsidies, with cultural contributions, with workers and soldiers, and with contemporary domestic social pluralism. Whatever the costs of these aids to the donors, Europe has benefited mightily.[1] But here, my subject is a more sharply focused look at how imperialism abroad, however much seen as beneficial to the national project, has been damaging to democratic efforts at home. The point of Orwell's short story was his realization that to rule others, we have to become sahibs. That is my historical argument as well.

This book is about how the system that made sahibs in the colonies produced correlate effects in the metropoles. I mean here more than so-called *blowback*—the name the CIA gave to unanticipated negative consequences at home of overseas actions, like how the United States trained the terrorists who we now fear. In his book of that name, Chalmers Johnson traces these undesired consequences of United States imperial strivings both for American overseas goals and for domestic politics. It is the book to read on that sort of imperial grotesquery.[2]

But what empires take away from democracies—are they really, always, and for certain unwanted by those who eye world power? Johnson's subsequent study, *The Sorrows of Empire*, comes to conclusions about larger backworkings of empire that, despite his focus on the United States in the contemporary world, support my own findings here about French and British colonialism. In his conclusion, he names "the loss of democracy" as a major sorrowful consequence of empire building.[3]

How did a systematic "sahibism," acclimated back home, become a permanently corrupting feature of certain Western democratic societies? Even thus delimited, the question is too big for one author and one book. The following chapters do not pretend to exhaust the catalogue of the negative heritage of colonialism in the West. For example, there is little here on racism, the militarization of Western societies, gender implications, or the question of immigrant workers.[4]

The colonial effect is like accumulating magma. So I have decided to do test borings at critical historical strata where the negative workings of imperial expansion on the growth of democratic society in metropolitan nations have been less understood and yet are accessible for study. To follow how I ground this claim in historical specifics, I invite you to trek with me across British, French, and American societies. Within Europe and America, in certain and specific ways, we will come on evidence of the real presence of nominally faraway places—of Burma, the Ivory Coast, India, Algeria, the Pacific Islands, and the stolen lands of the Amerindians.

I'm not the first person to have asked how empires affect their creators. Certain suggestive, but finally misleading, historical correlations between kinds of governments and overseas ambitions are periodically raised. Peter Padfield has recently recycled Britain's Admiral Jackie Fisher's passionate, if self-interested, belief that societies with large and powerful navies to protect home and colonies have avoided oppressive standing armies at home, a garrison state (like Sparta or Prussia), and so, an illiberal society. Writing from a different perspective, Eric Hobsbawm has remarked on the curious fact that the last great surge of nineteenth-century empire building was the affair of the most modern, most liberal, and potentially most democratic societies of the West. Britain, France, Holland, Belgium, and, I have to add, the United States not only began the strenuous practice of imperialism early in their statehood, but they also became the most successful practitioners of the so-called new imperialism of the late nineteenth century. After early strong showings, Spain and Portugal could not keep up with the more capitalist states in the modern imperial cross-country races. Nor did latecomers like Germany, the Austro-Hungarian Empire, Italy, Russia, or Japan do well.[5]

I do not think democracy is about navies, or Japan would have built a great democracy in the interwar years. Nor, from its creation in Bismarck's new empire to 1945, did the German Imperial High Seas Fleet —even though it was the darling of German nationalist liberals—prove anything but, first, the most reactionary and, then, the most nazified of the military services. And the Weimar Republic's weak and short existence was certainly not due to the support of merchant and banking patricians of Frankfurt, Hamburg, or Bremen. I think Hobsbawm is looking in the right places in noting the link between liberalism and empire. Like him, I am interested in the why of that covariation. And I am interested, as well, in how things turned out: that is, does democracy atrophy in a great empire? My answer is—finally—yes. But, I will argue, certain weaknesses of liberal capitalist and politically democratic societies have made empire a temptation, nay, a need—at least for the incumbent rulers. Clearly, we have a lot of traveling to do.[6]

The first leg of our trip takes us to the Ivory Coast and then on to Burma to meet two sahibs, a French colonial officer and a British policeman. These men who ran local areas of their respective modern empires were seen by their superiors as people of a special character. But not everyone had the right stuff to run a colony. In the beginning, most colonial powers practiced administrative bricolage. Trading companies like the East India Company, for example, in the case of Britain, and the navy in the instance of France, initially did the job. But because mistakes were made and because, taking its last big imperial bite in the latter half of the nineteenth century, Europe brought millions more under its rule, the major powers were obliged to create special corps for controlling their vast colonial possessions. Sometimes the administrators wrote interestingly about their work to maintain the empire, about what they learned, and how their jobs shaped their characters or their character shaped their jobs. And sometimes, while rummaging through old personnel records, the historian can come on treasures like personality profiles, drawn up by experts for teachers and supervisors, defining the best sort of person for the work.

The memoirs of Raymond Gauthereau, a French colonial administrator who in 1945 found himself posted to the Ivory Coast, contain a fascinatingly revealing episode about the vocation of men such as himself. It begins with local villagers repeatedly petitioning him to shoot rogue elephants foraging in their crops. Since the local people were not allowed arms, it fell on the local officers to keep the peace both in the human and the animal kingdoms. Since it is his job, Gauthereau finally decides he had better do it.

Gauthereau's account of the exploit is lifted from a similar incident that George Orwell narrates in his earlier story titled "Shooting an Elephant." Sometimes, rather than being a disappointing dead end, plagiarisms yield insights, as here, because the completely parallel yet differently nuanced stories put into relief this important quality "character" so valued in colonial officials. At the same time, we learn how the habitus of each—that meeting point of the social and the individual— were related to the differing cultural styles of their respective colonialisms. With difficulty, the French officer makes his kill—and learns from the event that he needs a better rifle. With even more trouble, Orwell also brings down his beast. But in doing so, he understands the corrupting force for Europeans of being a sahib—and that imperialism must end as much for the sake of the conquerors as for the conquered. Neither animal, it turned out, needed to be shot. Soon after his incident, Orwell quit the colonial service and came home to champion anti-imperialism and socialism. Gauthereau stayed on the job. Only after the dissolution of the empire did he return to France to become a novelist. Meanwhile, sixty-three of Gauthereau's colleagues also came home to become senior members of the Fifth Republic's newly created Ministry of Cultural Affairs. André Malraux, their new superior, charged them to do in France what they had done in Africa.[7] So here we see sahibism translated back to France as a renewed top-down state cultural regime.

While both in France and Britain some few, very often artists and writers, drew back in various creative ways from the evils of imperialism, the rulers of the two nations clung mightily to their imperial possessions. In France in particular, the Paris International Colonial Exposition of 1931 celebrated a Greater France (*une plus grande France*) as never before.[8] A few years later, at the moment of the triumph of the Popular Front—which did show empathy for the colonized—a wave of antifascist French patriotism to save "the culture," ironically declassified the people in the colonies from inclusion as part of the nation.

In the interwar years, the Musée de l'Ethnographie de Paris (Ethnographic Museum of Paris) possessed the most important French collection of objects from nonurban societies. For the most part they had been gathered in the course of empire building. However, one of the museum's halls was dedicated to the material culture of the provinces of France. During the Popular Front, when the museum was renamed Musée de l'Homme (Museum of Man), the hall of French folklore was separated out and given its own identity as the Musée National des Arts et Traditions Populaires (National Museum of Folk Arts and Traditions).

This line drawn between a museum dedicated to humankind, that is, so-called primitive societies, and one devoted to metropolitan France also divided contemporary social theory: folklorists studied the French provinces; ethnologists studied the colonies. For the history of French culture, René Descartes's bad move of taking mind and body apart has convinced me that once you take a whole apart—humankind in this instance—you have a devil of a time gluing the parts together again. Finally, as confirmed by the peace signed in 1962 recognizing an Algerian nation, the Algerian Front de Libération Nationale (National Liberation Front, FLN) said, in effect, "We accept that you think us different, that you will not accommodate us to the republic; we will leave." Empire seemed to require two social sciences, then: one for the dominated overseas and another for the managed at home. The lessons learned from domination heavily infected the policy social sciences in metropolitan France. A draftee and a teacher in Algeria during that war, sociologist Pierre Bourdieu made it his work—which was necessarily at the same time, scientific and political—to end this invidious division.

An us and not-us mentality grew in the arts of the 1930s too. Viewing certain films of Jean Renoir will take us from a France of poor migrant workers in early 1930s Provence to a slowly flowing river in an India just after independence. Even as the peoples of the colonies fought to escape their orientalist bamboo cage, the lands of the South continued to exercise the pull of an antimodernism that has so strongly marked the twentieth-century West.

While trying to formulate some ideas for my almost consecrated role of providing historical background for conferences organized by people in the arts—in this particular case, a conference on the films of Jean Renoir—I found the trajectory of the great filmmaker's work instructive for my own interests in how colonialism diminished French democratic culture. The conference was to focus on Renoir's political films of the 1930s. So, initially, I had intended on concentrating on the historical moment, the era of the Popular Front, when he made *La vie est à nous* (Our life belongs to us, 1936) and *La Marseillaise* (The Marseillaise, made in 1937 but released in 1938). I planned to end my paper with the evidence of his disenchantment with changing the rigid social hierarchy of France, his brilliant *La règle du jeu* (The rules of the game, 1939). But then I saw *Toni* (1934), an earlier film, and *The River* (1951), the film he made after World War II in English on location in India. Viewing all these films in the order of their making allowed me to see an arc of meaning connecting them, and another way in which empire functioned for Europeans.

Toni, which Renoir made just as the world depression hit France, tells a tale of backbreaking work and boiling human passions among quarry workers and peasants in the Midi. Most of the characters in the film are not French; they have curious accents, different customs, and uncommon names. But it does not matter—Renoir treats them as part of a larger humanity. No celebration here of the quaint and folkloric characters of the Midi as in the films of his contemporary Marcel Pagnol. Renoir demonstrates a great human empathy with these sejourners' hard lives, their exploitation on the job, and their intense, and finally fatal, loves. In *Toni* he shows sensitivity to the many ways of living in France.

The two expressly political films that followed *Toni*, namely, *La vie est à nous*, and *La Marseillaise*, were done at the moment of the Popular Front. In these, suddenly, Renoir very much cared about accents and nationality. For, each in its own way, was about who were the "real" French and who, like the contemporary two hundred richest families or Marie Antoinette and her German-speaking companions, were not. The us in *La vie est à nous* is the French working class. And in *La Marseillaise* it is the "little people" of Marseilles and Paris. Once the French aristocrats leave the country, they grow estranged from the living culture of the homeland they have abandoned. They, too, begin to risk joining the not-us.

Renoir made *La règle du jeu* after the defeat of the Popular Front and with it of his hopes for a new world of *fraternité*. About aristocrats and high bourgeois and their servants weekending on a large country estate, it takes the form of a comedy of manners. It features illicit loves and the games of the rich. Uncontained human passions prevoke a fatal shooting. But the film ends with the restoration of a violated order. After the "unfortunate accident," the marquis, the host, invites all—guests and servants—to return to the château.

After the war, and the declaration of Indian independence, Renoir left Los Angeles for India to make *The River*. With this work, we see his turning away from the public sphere entirely to celebrate the simplicity and calm of Indian village life, a surrogate of the world he had lost in France. The supposed inner peace of communal societies— recall, he made this film soon after the communal riots that killed and/or displaced hundreds of thousands at the moment of Pakistan and Indian statehood—had replaced for him and for many other tired Westerners the politicized and contested modernity of the urban West. Here is the third world figured as a slow river of peace and harmony, far from the new postwar struggles back in France to remake the metropole. No longer a champion of the little people of humankind as in *Toni* and his Popular Front films, Renoir aestheticized the timelessness, tranquility, and earthy passions in the peaceful countryside of the third world. He made political disengagement enchanting.

Finally, with the last three essays, I ask the terrible *Et alors?* question. That is, the hard question we sometimes pose to prolix doctoral students: "So what? Why are you telling me all this?" In these chapters, I move from the historical specifics of the first essays and try to develop a larger argument on how the modern Western democratic societies needed the colonial, used the colonial, and integrated the colonial into global capitalist modernity. The first two essays in this section are dedicated to the long-term colonial solutions to the most fundamental —for those who would rule—social problems at home: the risk of democracy and the dangers of modernity. The historical moments I have found illuminating are, first, Britain between the Puritan revolution and the one called glorious. Second, the imperial dimension of modernity came later, in mid-nineteenth century France, after the bloody suppression of the workers' revolution in 1848. In the first instance, I will ask a philosopher, John Locke, to explain to us how—by means of America—stable parliamentary government came to depend on capitalism and empire. In his turn, the great poet of modernity, Charles Baudelaire, points the way to understanding the rapports of aesthetic modernism and social modernity with the world of the tropics.

Rereading John Locke seems to me a good way to begin better to understand how this linkage of democratic aspiration and colonial rule came to be appreciated by the powerful men of the seventeenth century, and, in the case of Locke, their house philosophers.[9] If not the most brilliant theorist of liberal society, Locke was certainly its most successful apologist. In an early anticipation of the just-in-time system of capitalist production, the author had the *Two Treatises of Government* ready for delivery in 1688, just as the parliament was exiling Charles II and inviting William and Mary to rule Britain. He has since been celebrated as *the* philosopher of legislative prerogatives and a limited executive, the advocate of tolerance in a divided country. We owe to Locke the clearest philosophical explication of the imbrication of productive wealth and liberal government, of who had the right to rule. In 1647 during the heated ideological debates between some citizens and officers of Cromwell's army then camped at Putney outside London, Commissary-General Henry Ireton tried to stop discussion of this hot question raised by members of the lower ranks in the army by insisting that only people who owned property and so held "a permanent fixed interest in the kingdom," had a right to decide the course of the nation.[10] This formulaic reponse could not, and did not close, the debate. Too many people, some with weapons and a strong sense of entitlement, owned no property. Nor, unhappily, did they see how they might aspire to such ownership. During England's second regime change in the seventeenth century, Locke invoked empire—America—this open-ended, if tricky, entré to participatory politics at home, as his answer to this the most contested question of the modern age. It is right to speak of Locke as the godfather of all later social imperialists, everywhere.

Then to turn our attention to the sibling of imperial liberalism, its social correlative of literary modernism, we move forward some centuries to the France of Napoleon III and the moment of the great remaking of Paris. Walking distractedly in the vast fields of demolition and construction after the street fighting of 1848 and the start of the great reshaping of the city Charles Baudelaire formulated his new discourse on the modern. The poet's Black Venus became his guide, his modernist Beatrice, in the new uncharted world of Baron Georges-Eugène Haussmann's Paris. Since Baudelaire modernism has tempted overwrought artists and intellectuals of the democratic West with the offer of shelter in another, purer, world of art.

Then, to conclude, I will describe the path of historical inquiry toward a cultural history that could, finally, speak of colonial oppression and metropolitan change, without limiting our knowledge to only the slave trade, commerce, resource extraction, and illegal immigrants. My last essay, "Why, Suddenly, Are the Americans Doing Cultural History," was first published nearly ten years ago in a French social science review, in a "Controversy" section invented, as far as I can tell, just for me. It is about why so many progressive U.S. historians have diminished their interest in the social history of the 1960s to begin to do a new cultural history in the nineties. My French friends—and we remained friends despite this well-intentioned attempt at marginalizing my proposal that we on the Left do more cultural history—still sought in the life and work experiences of workers the key to their achieving radical consciousness. However, in the essay, I describe a move away from a limited theory of social organization and of social contestation—which seemed to me both an unnecessarily positivist and undialectical reading of Marx—to studies that appreciate how language, symbols, images, gender choices, and groups' identity claims serve as important modes of expressing refusal and resistance to unjust power. Taking from cultural anthropology important elements of theory initially fashioned to study empire, cultural history has become the preferred entry to the study of the metropole, the colonial, and the postcolonial. It is able to grasp the colonial situation and so speak of the connections and interactions between metropole and colonies in new ways. It is, I have found, a major means of understanding the historical effects of globalization on societies everywhere. As a personally guided tour through the discussions of the past several decades of how to do history, I thought it useful to mention at the end of that chapter a few of the key books, and to say something about their importance for taking us from there to here. I hope this readers' guide will help others take the next step in understanding our future.

Let us now start our own colonial adventure with an elephant hunt on the Ivory Coast.

ACKNOWLEDGMENTS

The chapters that follow originate in my longtime and many-sided interest in questions about "empires back home," the current shorthand phrase that describes the back workings of colonialism and imperialism on the metropolitan countries. All of them started life as invited lectures or conference papers. I gave part of Chapter 1,"Not the Right Stuff" in 2004 as a talk to the New York University Institute of French Studies. Chapter 2 was first invited by the Centre de Sociologie Euro-péenne as a contribution to the Colloque International des Sciences Sociales et Réflexivité: Hommage à Pierre Bourdieu held in Paris in January 2003, on the occasion of the one-year anniversary of its one-time director's death. It was entitled "Pierre Bourdieu et la crise post-coloniale des sciences sociales en France." I was privileged to be invited to give another part of the current chapter, also in Paris, later that year, as "Politique et folklore en France," at the Conference Du Folklore à l'Ethnologie sponsored by the Musée National des Arts et Traditions Populaires. Chapter 3, on Jean Renoir, was written for a conference on the filmmaker and then published as a special number of *The Persistence of Vision,* a film studies review published at the City University of New York (CUNY) Graduate Center. Chapter 4, on aesthetic modernism and colonialism, was presented in 2001 both in the lecture series The Nation and Beyond, held at the Center for Historical Studies, University of Maryland, College Park and, on the invitation of the graduate student members, to the French Cultural Studies seminar series at the University of Pennsylvania. Chapter 5, on Locke as imperialist thinker, which I was invited to give at the Third Centenary of the Publication of the *Two Treatises of Government* sponsored by the Clarendon Edition of the Works of John Locke, the British Society for the History of

Acknowledgments

Philosophy, the Subfaculty of Philosophy, and Christ Church, Oxford, at Christ Church, Oxford, on 5 September 1990 appeared in an early version in 1986 in the *Journal of the History of Ideas* as "The Uses of America in John Locke's Second Treatise. Chapter 6, on why we do cultural history, I've been revising and updating for presentation as the introduction to my graduate seminar on the issues and methods of cultural history. (I suppose that's not technically an invited lecture, perhaps the contrary.) It also appeared in an early draft in 1995 as "Une 'nouvelle histoire culturelle'? La politique de la différence chez les historiens américains," in the journal *Genèses: Sciences sociales et histoire.* I wish to thank the editors of the three publications for permission to adapt and use these pieces here. Chapters 1, 2, and 4 have never before been published, although certainly critiqued.

I have rewritten all the essays in the volume—previously published or not—and brought the discussions and bibliographies up to date. Reading them over *together*, as I have had to do, yielded new ideas and insights, which I added to the pieces and especially to the preface and the afterword. I hope the reader might find the whole greater than the sum of its parts as well.

Thanks to the helpful readings of the book manuscript by Edward Berenson and an anonymous reader. Thanks also, and again, to the literary and people skills of Valerie Millholland of Duke University Press. I cannot begin to thank all my friends, readers, listeners, and critics who, over the many years of their composition, helped me perfect these chapters. Rather than leave off any names, let me just embrace the practice of some French authors who justify their intellectual borrowings without acknowledgments or footnotes with: they will know who they are.

Finally, again, as with *Bringing the Empire Back Home,* a word of thanks for the aid and friendship of Danielle Haase-Dubosc, Brune Biebuyck, and Mihaela Bacou of the Columbia University Center for Scholars and Reid Hall, where in the summer of 2005 I completed work on this volume. Together in the historical arts district of Montparnasse they have fashioned an atelier in which artisan scholars like myself have been able to do some of our best work.

MAISON SUGER
Paris, June 2005

1

NOT THE RIGHT STUFF

Shrinking Colonial Administrators

Raymond Gauthereau, a new district officer, arrived in 1945 in the French colony of the Ivory Coast. In the book of memoirs he wrote about his service, he devoted a few pages to his shooting a marauding elephant.[1] The passage reads very much like a set piece. After he left the colonial service, Gauthereau turned to writing novels, and thus he had some practice in literary invention. It is unlikely that there is any truth to the story. Yet its invention tells us more about the history of colonial administration, and of its dissolution, than if it had been a true report of a real event.

Three times in two weeks the villagers of Krakou had sent emissaries to request that he do something about a marauding herd of elephants. A group of about thirty had moved into the district and were ravaging their crops. Coming very close to the village itself, they threatened to turn a hut over or even hurt someone. It had happened before. The villagers had no arms. Even the native constables were not issued ammunition for their old rifles. So all depended on him.

Gauthereau had hesitated to act. The local people exaggerated so in their accounts of events. They had an appetite for the "big meat" (*grosse viande*) (165) that a downed elephant would add to their diet. And then to do a wild-animal kill he needed to seek the explicit consent of the governor-general, a man far away, with whom he had had

A still from Jean-Jacques Annaud's film *Black and White in Color* (1976) of a Naval Infantry (Marine) Officer of the type who administered colonies before trained colonial administrators replaced them. Author's collection.

very little contact up to now. Finally, the villagers sent a delegation, led this time by two small coffee growers who were black veterans of World War I clad in their old uniforms, "which had been blue before becoming gray" (166). These old *tirailleurs* had not entirely forgotten their French. As evidence of the damage suffered, they brought along half-eaten plants and sticks, some nearly sixteen inches (forty centimeters) thick, that the elephants had broken.

All right, Gauthereau would have a look. He had never shot an animal. Big-game hunters in his district had offered to take him along on one of their authorized tourist shoots, but he had refused. Shooting a big animal was "an adventure that I wanted to deflower alone" (167). He wrote the governor-general asking permission for an "official kill" (167).

While still waiting for the telegram authorizing the hunt, his immediate chief suddenly turned up unannounced. Or, rather, he showed up before the telegram informing the young district officer of the visit arrived. It was his superior's first tour since Gauthereau had been posted to the district. The man did a turn of inspection of the compound—the maternity clinic, the prison—said a few words of encouragement, and left. Clearly, his boss had nothing to tell him; Gauthereau was on his own. As he narrated the sudden visit and quick departure of his superior, Gauthereau took a moment to meditate on how he had had to learn his job by himself. His training at the École Coloniale was not what he thought most important. Rather, he had learned on the job to act "with prudence, good sense, a regard to justice, and the judicious alternation of severity and amiability—and above all, with patience. And, by God, I haven't screwed up yet" (167).

Finally, after three weeks of waiting, the permission arrived. Gauthereau tells the tale as a flashback, in the après-hunt mode. Sitting at his table, cleaned up, bathed, fed, and relaxed, he writes in his diary, "Today, I, who have never hunted before . . . killed an elephant" (178). It had taken a whole day, nearly thirty-five kilometers of walking, and seven shots (admittedly with ordinary-issue ammunition, not heavy rounds), but he had gotten his kill.

When he had arrived at the village to begin the hunt, the people greeted him with great enthusiasm. The herd had moved on by now, no longer posing a threat. But, he lets us understand, the villagers were still eager for their banquet, as well as for their revenge on the beasts. They had sent out trackers who soon picked up the freshest trail of the herd. There was no way out; the villagers expected him to shoot an elephant. For Gauthereau this posed a series of technical problems—beginning with the question of his competence as a hunter—but no moral issue about killing what were now harmless wild animals.

Early the next morning, the whole village assembled to urge him on with so much enthusiasm and confidence "that there was no question of my coming back without a kill, except at the price of losing face" (179). With a village tracker and his "least bad musketeer" (179) from the post, he set out on the forest path to save his honor. In the course of the long walk, the two Africans quarreled a lot about the signs and what they meant, but also just to quarrel, according to Gauthereau. The villager was a Gouro (a southern Mandé population) with "too hard a head," (180) according to the pidgin French of his constable, Dosso, a Muslim from another group. So, in a cameo of the imperial alibi, he, the white colonial officer, had to enforce peace between the two, ethnically different, feuding Africans.

Suddenly, in a clearing, they spotted a single elephant. Without much fanfare, Gauthereau raised his rifle and put a shot into the animal's heart. He did not aim for the head because the ammunition he had in his standard-issue rifle was too low powered to penetrate the thick bone of the skull. Surprised, the animal started, and then began to run. Gautherau shot again, with no apparent results. Following the trail of blood, the three men ran after the wounded animal. Again, they got close enough. Despite the advice the experts had given him, Gauthereau sent his next two shots into the head. The elephant seemed not to be weakening. And Gauthereau, despite having done a lot of sports, was getting tired chasing it. He was winded, dehydrated, and almost exhausted. He had fallen several times during the chase. To keep going he reminded himself that, in a similar situation, his friend, the white hunter Denkel, had not failed. The pursuit continued. As he strained, Gauthereau held desperately to his conviction that a well-conditioned white could keep up with a black in the forest.

It began to get dark. Finally, just an hour before nightfall, they came on the middle-sized, perhaps three-ton (metric) male, standing as if awaiting his inevitable fate. Gauthereau moved in close and fired three more rounds. The elephant raised his trunk, fell to his knees, and died.

Dosso approached the fallen animal and more or less symbolically—the skin was so thick—cut its throat in good orthodox Muslim fashion. Suddenly, men from the village appeared in the clearing. They had trailed discreetly behind, and then, following the sounds of the shots of the final kill, had closed in. Holding torches, knives, and machetes, a dozen of them stood around the huge mass of flesh lying on the ground. Dosso persuaded them to wait until the next morning to butcher the animal. It was getting dark. It would be better to go back to the village. The men agreed, but not before cutting off the two choice morsels of the trunk and the testicles—this latter, according to Gauthereau, appreciated locally as a "delicacy, rich in beneficial qualities" (183). They left a guard to protect the meat from the "cupidity" of people from other villages and headed back. When Gauthereau arrived back at Krakou, they honored him "with a triumph" (183).

To end his diary entry—which, after all, as a literary exercise needed a strong finish—Gauthereau offers us his meditations on his experience. He confesses to having mixed feelings. The adventure had been exciting, but it could have been more so had he known more about tracking and hunting. He had found the actual kill a bit disgusting. He makes no mention of the herd that was still out there, nor even of the by no means certain connection of this shot elephant to the damaged crops. What had he learned from the drama? If he had had to do it all over again, "it would be with a rifle powerful enough to avoid another marathon chase—and to reduce the elephant's suffering" (183).

This is how he concludes his morality tale about colonial rule and personal competence—that is, he shows us not very competent Africans and a French administrator who proves himself. It is at the same time a tale in which expertise and technical skills have the most important value—the operation of a telegraph needing improvement, the skill and conditioning of the shooter, the quality and caliber of the firearms. This is a vision of African colonialism as a series of administrative and technical problems, narrated as a self-celebration of the machismo of a proconsul of the empire who overcame them. For added effect, he gratuitously sneers at the people. It is the story of the two logics of contemporary colonialism: the disjunction between the deeply premodern values of the administrator and his taste for technological modernity. It is just what the champions of empire's separation of cognition from feelings that in his *Passage to India* E. M. Forster called the "undeveloped heart."

ANOTHER ELEPHANT KILL

From the literary point of view, Gauthereau's is not a very interesting or well-told story. But, then, most writers are not George Orwell. It is clear that Gauthereau modeled his tale after Orwell's famous story "Shooting an Elephant."[2] In fact, the similarities between the two events are so striking that I would hazard the judgment that Gauthereau's never happened; or if it did, it was nothing like what he described. Orwell's was written long before Gauthereau published his memoirs; it was a well-known short story, at least in the English-reading world. That is probably where Gauthereau found his elephant, or most of it. Orwell's incident did not happen the way he tells it either, although his biographer Bernard Crick has found good evidence that he did in fact shoot an elephant while in the Burma police.[3] But the two *stories* written about killing an elephant, stories we can compare, are certainly historical facts.

The two accounts both play on the killing-the-dragon variant of the lone-champion literary convention. They are both tales of an untried hero, surrounded by expectant, weak, but judgmental onlookers, who has to prove himself by killing a great, terrifying beast. Although poorly armed, the (white) champion, after much travail, prevails. In the two stories the scenes leading up to the killings have many features in common. The action of the hunters, of the elephants, even those of the local people are described in very similar fashion, sometimes using the same words or images. Both stories are about a European saving face before the native people he rules and so protecting imperial hegemony. In both Orwell and, following him, in Gauthereau, the figure of the elephant becomes a trope for the dark unknown mass of the colonized, a great force of nature that if trained properly, remains mostly tranquil and normally hardworking. But sometimes the same people can rebel explosively and then prove dangerous. And from the experience of shooting an elephant, each account draws important lessons for the colonial officer and the colonial enterprise. But there, Orwell and Gauthereau diverge. Let us look at the Orwell story more closely.

A young officer in the Burmese colonial police is called on to stop a marauding elephant. The creature had gone into heat, "must," and had broken his chain. He was rampaging about town. A Burmese sub-inspector across town asked the narrator—hereafter referred to as "Orwell" although the author does not give him a name—to deal with the matter.[4] "The Burmese population had no weapons and were quite helpless against it" (16–17). Taking his carbine—actually, a Winchester 44, the rifle made famous for having conquered the indigenous peoples of the American West—Orwell went out to look for the animal. When he came to the bazaar, where the animal had last been seen, he could

George Orwell (still Eric Blair), third from left, back row, with fellow officers of the Burma police, 1923. With the permission of University College London Library Services, Orwell Archive.

not get a very coherent story from the local people about where it had gone: "This is invariably the case in the East (17). . . . I had almost made up my mind that the whole story was a pack of lies, when we heard yells a little distance away" (17). Walking in that direction, he came on the body of a black Dravidian coolie, whom the charging elephant had crushed. His grotesque corpse had been trampled deep into the mud, the skin on his back flayed off in strips by the scrapping of the elephant's foot. On seeing what this animal could do, Orwell sent an orderly to a friend's house for an elephant gun. The soldier quickly returned with the weapon and five cartridges.

Soon, some Burmese came to tell him that the elephant was now grazing in a field a few hundred yards away. He started in the direction they indicated. Now he was being followed by what appeared to be the whole population of the quarter, with more and more people swelling the crowd as he walked. They were relishing the entertainment in the offing and "they wanted the meat" (18). They wanted the kill, and at the same time they wanted the British policeman to fail. But above all, as Orwell realized, as he stood alone deciding whether to shoot or not, they were the ones in charge.

When he got to the animal, it was peacefully grazing in a paddy field, not far from the road. "As soon as I saw the elephant I knew with perfect certainty that I ought not to shoot him. It is a serious matter to shoot a working elephant—it is comparable to destroying a huge and costly piece of machinery" (18–19). Besides, clearly the attack of must was wearing off. The animal would now graze quietly until his mahout came to get him.

But, to the general delight of the now perhaps two thousand spectators, Orwell did shoot. The first shot surprised the animal. He had aimed well. The elephant sank slowly to his knees. But the second hit seemed to revive him. At least, he stood up again. The third jolted his body. You could see it. The wounded creature raised his trunk and trumpeted a single time, and then fell full length to the ground. "He was dying, very slowly and in great agony" (22). To finish him, Orwell fired his last two bullets into where he thought the creature's heart might be. But it would not die faster. He then took up his lower caliber rifle, the Winchester, and put shot after shot into the heart and, through its open mouth, down the throat of the animal. The young officer could not stand the slow dying. He walked away. A half hour afterward, he heard later, it finally died. "Burmans were bringing dahs [knives] and baskets even before I left, and I was told they had stripped his body almost to the bone by the afternoon" (22).

The French colonial administrator sees his act as a vindication of the colonial tasks he had been sent to do. In killing his elephant, Orwell discovers the terrible secret of colonialism for the rulers: it enslaves them to the people they oppress. In telling us about how he went about his job, Orwell also speaks of his prior disenchantment with British imperialism. Even before he had to kill the harmless elephant before the cheering crowd, he had already decided that "imperialism was an evil thing" (15). He was ready to quit the Burma police service. But this hunt taught him something new about himself as one of the rulers. Colonial rule destroyed the freedom of the governors. The role they had to assume made them the stick figures in a colonial drama. He had

Eric Blair (later George Orwell), aged six weeks, in the arms of his Indian ayah, 1903. With the permission of University College London Library Services, Orwell Archive.

stood there in the field certain that the animal, now calm, need not be killed,

> And suddenly I realized that I would have to shoot the elephant after all. The people expected it of me and I had got to do it; I could feel their two thousand wills pressing me forward, irresistibly. And it was at this moment, as I stood with the rifle in my hands, that I first grasped the hollowness, the futility of the white man's domination in the East. . . . In reality I was only an absurd puppet pushed to and fro by the will of these yellow faces behind. I perceived at this moment that when the white man turns tyrant it is his own freedom that he destroys (19).

The white man becomes a posing sahib. And "a sahib has got to act like a sahib; he has got to appear resolute, to know his own mind, and do the definite thing" (20). With all those people watching, Orwell could not just put down his rifle and walk away. He had to do the kill or be considered weak. The people he should rule would laugh at him. "And my whole life, every white man's life in the East, was one long struggle not to be laughed at" (20).

That is why Orwell had to shoot the now calm elephant, and that is why, after a herd had done some damage, Gauthereau had to kill the first elephant that came into his gun sights. But where Orwell deeply understood how imperialism had cost not just the freedom of the ruled people but also his own, Gauthereau's head was cluttered only with worries about his manliness, about not embarrassing himself before the natives, and about the quality of his firearms. He doesn't get it.

BEHIND THE METAPHOR

Many citizens of democracies whose nation takes on colonial rule do not understand the cost to freedom *at home*. It is, in fact, systematically *mis*understood, like the French administrator's lack of insight into what was really at stake about his role in the hunt, about France's role in Africa, and about Africa's role in France. It is hard to find a better illustration of the difference between instrumental reasoning—Gauthereau's sort of technocratic shoot—and normative reasoning—Orwell's understanding about why he was morally obliged to leave the Burmese police service for his own sake as much as for that of the people he ruled.

Although both men had been sent as colonial proconsuls by representative governments, colonial rule harked back to a lost ancien régime. At least it was disappearing in the European nations. The resituating—even revival—of aristocratic Britain in the colonial empire is a well-known story. Most recently, David Cannadine's *Ornamentalism* plays it again.[5] But the many commentators on French imperialism have seen colonialism as a modernist project. Metropolitan French society was increasingly gridlocked; but social experiments, in city planning, architecture, administration, medicine, social science, and, of course, military matters were possible in the empire.

The empire functioned as a proving ground for modern techniques of social control, doubtless. That was its instrumental side. But this much-repeated axiom misses a deeper current of colonial rule, its normative logic. The latest French colonialism, although a child of the

Third Republic, became also, and perhaps more importantly, a project of both modern conservatives and nostalgic republicans to reproduce in the colonies the world they had lost in metropolitan France. The social conservatives of the Action Française and of the Provençal revival of the late nineteenth century had, at the same time, played the same move with the provinces of France. Because of the historic role of the British Empire as the provision of "outdoor relief" for unemployed aristocrats, Orwell understood that to do the job, he had to take on a persona of paternalistic domination first defined during the British ancien régime and brought up to date in Burma, India, and Africa. But, despite the vulnerability of the new regime awaking in France and colonial revolts breaking out in several places in France Overseas, Gauthereau did not seem to know or care about the implications for the persistence of democracy in France of what he did in Africa.[6]

Farmers populated Gauthereau's story, as they filled the dominant French-colonial vision of the African colonies. Robert Delavignette—of whom more below—from the mid-1930s to the 1950s, the most influential republican theorist of colonial rule, championed recognition and respect for the different civilizations of the overseas empire (the postwar French Union). But for him these were peasant civilizations rooted in the land.[7]

Orwell's story, by contrast, features a—I would say—classic urban mob intimidating a policeman and making him yield to its will. Orwell confesses to a complicated emotional rapport with the people he policed. In fact, his story begins with, "In Moulmein, in lower Burma, I was hated by large numbers of people. . . . The young Buddhist priests were the worst of all. None of them seemed to have anything to do except to stand on street corners and jeer at Europeans" (15). No alienation effect working here. Orwell reacted with an irresolvable ambivalence. "With one part of my mind I thought of the British Raj as an unbreakable tyranny. As something clamped down . . . upon the will of prostrate peoples; with another part I thought that the greatest joy in the world would be to drive a bayonet into a Buddhist priest's guts" (16). We should note his attitude toward the priests was still a human one: he hated them, even as he wanted them to be free. They were awful fellow human beings who in expressing their hostility to the colonial rulers made his life miserable. He had no choice but to get out.

Gauthereau's mode is Olympian irony. The African soldiers, the villagers, African societies as a whole are bumptious infants. Although we learn in passing that they come from different tribes and have different cultural practices—ritually slaughtering the elephant, for example—Gauthereau offers us not much more on the identity of the peasants in his story. These villagers pose administrative problems, but their humanity holds little interest for the French official. They very much resemble the troublesome but finally malleable schoolchildren in the provincial France of the Third Republic, and he is their ever patient, if distant, schoolmaster. As for provincial schoolchildren, an authoritarian, if patronizing, style seems right for the Africans too. A democratic social order would never work out here.[8]

These two stories put in relief the conservative role played by the kind of anthropology that was encouraged especially by the British colonial authorities—in the 1950s given the name of structural functionalism—which allowed for a style of rule that accepted and used local beliefs and practices rather than disrespecting or thwarting them, or just using force. The French, compared to the British and, certainly, the Dutch, did much less to try to learn how local societies in their empire worked. Generally, they preferred to govern their African colonies with blanket policies and laws, admittedly tailored a bit to the societies being ruled.[9] The British colonial administrators, with the help of the anthropologists—but not George Orwell's policeman— kept order by learning and using the culture of the ruled, against them, as it were. In extremis, colonial authorities had to call on men with guns to kill indigenous rampaging animals and other sowers of troubles. But normally both the British and the French colonial government put the greatest responsibility for maintaining the empire on the shoulders of isolated (geographically and/or emotionally) colonial officers, who had to find inside themselves the will to rule.[10]

Although we have tales set at different times, on different continents, about different empires, they both culminate in the death of a great animal. In an urban part of southern Burma, the elephant was domesticated and normally docile in the work of reproducing the colonial order. But the sexual wildness in the animal could not be entirely suppressed. It was as if the emancipatory power of sexual energy in humans—which decades later Herbert Marcuse had so many hopes for—were to surface in the animals working in a colonial-capitalist world. Later in his life, the author of *Animal Farm* would use animals to tell another tale about human social liberation and its thwarting.

The town where Orwell's story is set was a major teak-exporting center. Elephants were crucial in the heavy work. After the kill—Orwell, the writer, really did shoot an elephant—the firm of Steel Brothers lodged a complaint with his superiors against Eric Blair (Orwell's birth name). This big British company that owned the animals, not some poor local person. In Burma the colonial companies had great influence with the administration; the young policeman was transferred to an undesirable posting in the north of Burma. To boot, his superior, one Colonel Welbourne, called him "a disgrace to Eton College."[11]

The other elephant, in French West Africa, was even wilder and more uncontrolled. It—or herds of them—could do harm to the unarmed farmers. In parts of French Africa elephants were protected by game laws so as not to tempt the villagers to become dependent on hunted food—and to save the animals for the European hunter-tourists.

In each story, the need to shoot the wild animal comes to mean the failure of the colonial project. More and more, force replaces so-called rational administration. Control of a situation that might bring discredit to colonial rule and to maintaining the agents of rule in their sahib status required both Gauthereau and Orwell to do a killing they knew was wrong. And both kills were messy—they foreshadowed botched colonial rule. Neither colonial officer's gun was powerful enough to do the job right. Now, of course, we could see in these performance failures Freudian flaccid penises. But I find the inadequacy of force to carry out the colonial project a more interesting reading of the lack of firepower the two shooters tell about. One of the district officers—the man who became a great socialist moralist—had the insight to see in his act the exhaustion of the colonial project. The other—a fiction writer in his next career—could not think the unthinkable and so fretted about technological means and ends. Let us look more closely at some other manifestations of the falling apart of the sense of mastery and self-justification of some other French colonial administrators working at the cusp of decolonization in the postwar years.

BACK TO THE GOLDEN AGE OF
THE COLONIAL SERVICE

Seen from above, from the perspective of their superiors, both Orwell's and Gauthereau's stories evidence the demoralization of the servants of empire. If Orwell is clear in his own mind about the nature of his disenchantment, Gauthereau's piece must be read more symptomatically. And in the postwar, at least in France, those charged with governing the empire did understand that a serious problem festered in the ranks. The administration weighed two responses. The first aimed at bringing serving officers back to a sense of responsibility; their superiors wanted to get the misguided officers back on track. The other solution required better monitoring of the recruitment of new officers. Directors of imperial rule asked themselves if the service was attracting men made of the right stuff. This second course proposed a more scientific approach, embracing modern personality psychology.

Considering that the colonial administrator operated mostly alone with his responsibilities, it was not unreasonable for his superiors to wish him to have the right character for his post. This was not new. Since the classical age, *character* was a concept early observers of overseas societies employed to describe and classify the new people they encountered. *Character* was used in the sense of national character, that is, asking what the Peules of Senegal were like, or the Iroquois of the New World.[12] As anthropological knowledge became richer and more sophisticated, the concept returned more to its older meaning in French society of an individual of virtue or lack thereof, although, as we saw from Gauthereau's account, a native group's "character" became an easy quasi-racial way to think about the people the empire administered.[13] And colonial officers lacking the right character were seen as a great problem in the post–World War II years.

Pierre Messmer himself graduated from the École Coloniale, attending the school from 1934 to 1937. A Gaullist resistant of the first hour he signed up as a Foreign Legion officer in the Free French military. He did most of his fighting in Africa and the Middle East. At the war's end, he returned once again to doing various missions in the colonial administration. In the years 1948–49, when the colonial empire was becoming France d'Outre-Mer (France Overseas), he took up the ad hoc post of chief administrator (*administrateur en chef*) of France d'Outre-Mer. From this vantage point he experienced and reacted to what he saw as both a moral and morale crisis that the corps of colonial administrators as a group was suffering. By 1956, when he worked for the minister of Overseas France, pragmatic ex–African administrator that he was, Messmer would accept the inevitability of decolonization. But in the immediate postwar years, he saw fixing the broken colonial administration as the best remedy for the current malaise of colonial officers.[14]

The continuation of the empire, he believed, depended on the well-functioning of the handful of widely scattered men supported by little in the way of infrastructure or strong military force. He understood that if the will to rule and the will to serve disappeared in the corps, the empire, or France d'Outre-Mer, would be lost to the local demagogues waiting in the wings, or, perhaps, in some places already on stage. He was receiving many requests for transfers back to France or to some big city in an overseas territory. Some administrators were overstaying their leaves. Other officers were requesting transfers to other services. In the lower ranks, confidence in the chain of command was waning, evidenced by a certain cynicism about the motives and capacities of their superiors. (Recall Gauthereau's not very flattering description of his chief's visit.) The same skepticism had led administrators to playing it safe. Increasingly, they just followed written orders, rather than, as in the past, taking initiatives and taking advantage of their great freedom of action. People were advanced or held back in the service, not on merit, but, in those highly politicized postwar years, because of influence or changes in the government.

The defeat of France in 1940, followed by the conflict between Vichy and Gaullist governments, had left a legacy of serious internal divisions in the colonial administration. In the postwar, France tried to change, to soften, to encourage more representative regimes in some of the colonies, as in parts of Africa and the Antilles. Independence movements in others, like in Indochina, were gaining strength. These regions were on the way to breaking away. Just before he had taken up this post, Messmer had parachuted into Indochina to try to keep it French. He had been captured by the Viet Minh who held him for some months before releasing him. He knew personally how desperate the situation was. The changes in the former empire after 1945 had "created the painful impression [in their ranks] that the cadre of colonial administrators was destined for a slow death."[15] And he realized the demoralizing nature of these changes for the older members of the service. They missed the old days; they were used to ruling. Those were the historic reasons for the malaise.

But the new cohorts (*nouvelles générations*) had not remained unaffected. The old standard of a service above politics, he says, had given way to a highly partisan one. The corps had become deeply divided into factious political tendencies. Good Gaullist that he was, he judged, "Such a situation is incompatible with maintaining the authority of the State, and risks, if it continues, having disastrous effects on the Overseas Territories."[16]

The crisis in morale and morality must be addressed quickly and effectively. First, he wanted the administration to get back in charge of itself: there had to be a return to the service's normal rules of promotion and sanctions. No more external political commitments or interference should be permitted. Depoliticize decision making in the administration, he insisted. Let the best, not the best connected, be advanced. And, returning to the old principle of French public life—the strict separation of the personal from the professional—he believed inquiries into the personal life of the cadre—"how they spend their salaries, do they have an automobile or a mistress, do they frequent the Bibliothèque Nationale or existentialist taverns"—should cease. The personal was not to be political in the colonial service. Give the administrators a free hand once again, he urged, return their local power, encourage their "tours of inspection in the bush," allow them their "palavers." Stop giving them the work of clerks. And finally, reward them for learning the customs, the economic conditions, the language of the people of the district. Reward them for the studies they publish. "These are the necessary conditions to stop the crisis—a potentially fatal one—which the corps of administrators has been suffering for the last ten years."

Reminding the people of the colonial administration of their duties when their demoralizing arose from the very loud not-said in Messmer's note—the impatience for change of the colonialized—does not seem a fully adequate response to the crisis. Perhaps a bit of introspection might have helped.

THE COLONIAL ADMINISTRATORS
HAVE THEIR HEADS SHRUNK

In the archives of last director of the École Coloniale, Robert Delavignette, may be found a curious document entitled "Le métier d'administrateur des colonies" ("The Métier of the Colonial Administrator").[17] It is a memorandum, or perhaps *essay* might be the better word, on what personal traits make for the best colonial administrator. Although it bears no date, it was almost certainly written in the immediate post–World War II years. It was commissioned by Jacques Christol, *directeur des affaires politiques*, in what after the war, but before decolonization, was called the Ministère de la France d'Outre-Mer. There existed a rich tradition of French colonial administrators seeking to tailor French rule to their ideas of *the* psychology of the ruled populations. While serving as head of education in Morocco, for example, Georges Hardy regularly pronounced on the presumed psychology of the Moroccans, and structuring their education accordingly.[18] But psychologizing the psychologizers is rare; I know of no other such document of French colonial administration—or any other country's colonial service —except this one on the model personality of a successful officer of empire.

The analysis shows a familiarity with aspects of Freudianism, suggesting that it was written by a psychological professional. Presumably Delavignette had been sent the psychological profile to guide him in assessing applicants and students at the École Coloniale. Was it ever used in any way to filter or judge present or future administrators? I found no direct evidence to answer that question. But the guidelines were sent by one of the highest officials of the colonial administration to the head of the training school for new colonial officers. So "The Métier of the Colonial Administrator" must remain one of those rich texts that perhaps, reversing what Stephen Greenblatt has done so well, we can use to guide our history writing without attributing empirical truth value to its contents. The fact that it had to be written at all, and the symptoms of malaise in the colonial service we can detect from its concerns, make it a valuable historical document.

Why should a high official of the colonial administration feel it necessary, in the years just after the liberation of France, to try to reimpose control over the empire, to write this not very bureaucratic document and send it to at least one key official involved in assessing the psychic makeup of the rulers of empire? What did this official and, as we can judge from the marginal annotations by Delavignette, the head of the training school who agreed with his thoughts think was the ideal personality of a successful district officer? Or put another way, once the crisis in French colonial rule is addressed as a psychological crisis of the men who run the empire, can the end of empire be far off?

How to get colonial administrators to love their work? How to harmonize their psychic needs and satisfactions with their tasks? The author of "Le métier d'administrateur des colonies" refers to this habitus—this conjunction of personality with organizational tasks—as the "'Persona.'" Orwell preferred the more pointed term *sahib*. But both the profile and Orwell mark the same psychic territory.

The commander of a territory that could have as many as three hundred thousand or four hundred thousand people under his control (*administrés*) must above all be able to rule. But how to rule? By obeying what can only be called the imperial superego: "If we compare the governed territory to a human being, the man in charge would be the conscience of this great body: a conscience that understands its needs and desires, that has a will to action guided by a precise moral rule." In practice, this means that the good colonial administrator must know how to punish. He must have so internalized "a sense of social justice" that he will not be torn between his subjective feelings and his duties when he must act against breaches of authority. "If the administrator is in rebellion against all social authority, he would be inclined to identify with those who also manifest this sentiment, and so would be out of line with his professional obligations which require him to sanction this kind of activity." This formulation, let me point out, is an outrageous, if frequently employed, abuse of psychology to pathologize sentiments of rebellion as antisocial behavior. The successful administrator should feel no empathy with rebels. Nor should he allow himself any sympathy with their cause. He must fully believe in the legitimacy of command

and subordination. He must embrace the established order and be prepared to defend it as "sacred, or out of sincere love of it, or out of self-interest." The memorandum goes on, "The ability to think this way can be found especially among individuals in whom the 'moi' has remained at the religious stage of emotional development. That is, the moi submits to social authority like the infant submits to the Father and the believer to God." With this psychic makeup, the administrator will obey his superiors in the service, who, after all, represent the highest authority, the state.[19] We should not think that manifestation of this religious stage indicates a regression. Few humans—even very few scientists—are capable of real scientific thought: "Humanity today has an emotional age of a twelve or thirteen year old, so the religious *mentalité* [state of mind] is in no way a regression."

What are the psychological forces that inculcate the sense of duty an administrator takes with him when all alone he journeys deep into the bush? There are many: conditioning to obedience in infancy, fear of abandonment by loved ones or social group, an inferiority complex vis-à-vis authority, and above all, a sense of guilt. Even the sublimation of sexual desire into a love of duty—serving a republic that, after all, is symbolized by a young woman—can be another tie to duty. Admittedly, this last constitutes a "peculiar kind of fetishism," but nevertheless, it can make for a profound source of motivation. But one must also pay attention, so that these forces creating a sense of duty do not become too much for the individual, for the *moi*, and so produce neurotic symptoms. An inferiority complex that crushes the individual, too strong a sense of guilt, failed sublimation, latent masochism—all these must be avoided.

But how to balance between desires and obligations, a question Freud wrestled with all his life? The author of the memorandum has an easy answer. His tone changes; he takes up the *manly* mode: Do not take all this advice too seriously. Everything must be tempered with a sense of humor, in the British way. If not, the neurotic behavior of the administrator will deprive the organization of his talents.

A well-balanced administrator should be motivated by humanism, originating in his identifying, to a degree, with the governed. He should be aware that he brings them a superior civilization from Europe. They—"the backward peoples"—should in turn see their obligation as trying to profit from these contributions to make up for lost time, and so themselves someday to arrive at the level of civilization. The author is fond of repeatedly invoking the word *Gulliverian* as a metaphor for the colonial relationship.

The administrator should not lose sight of this cultural divide. He must want to help those he rules, but he must be motivated by his strong sense that he knows better and has better things to offer them than they possess. Some—there are very few, the writer thinks—have argued that an administrator in the colonies might well be seen as, say, an official born in the Auvergne stationed in Alsace and who simply enforces regulations among people whose customs are different from his own region, but who follow the rules "exactly like a peasant in France submits to the rules presented to him by the tax collector." No, this is wrong-headed. In a piece of megabad faith, the author responds that equating administering France at home and France overseas re-fuses to acknowledge the "interpsychological problems of colonialism." As if the asymmetries of colonial power were founded on psychological differences!

But, empathetic though he be, the administrator must resist, finally, an overly strong sense of identification with the autochthones. He must realize, like the Christian missionary, the superiority of, in his case, the science of nature, of what he brings to the colonized. "It is good to keep this in mind because many Europeans today have an inferiority com-plex vis-à-vis the Africans. . . . If we have nothing to contribute, noth-ing to give, no reason to make the effort, to dedicate ourselves, it is perfectly useless to be an administrator."

So, all the psychological preparation—the creation of a habitus whereby duty becomes a personal desire, and the will to serve the highest fulfillment of self—is to do good. You would not think you needed to develop characters something like those of Spartans or Jesu-its to be a "Samaritan" (the author's word) toward fellow human beings in Africa and Asia. Yet you do need men of this sterner stuff to try to avoid the disintegration of a colonial empire more and more recog-nized, even in metropolitan France, as oppressive and illegitimate. And if the growing "inferiority complex" (read sense of wrongdoing) of Europeans before their crimes in the colonies were to spread—obviously was spreading—to the cadre assigned to colonial rule, how would continued colonial rule be possible? The fighting in Indochina and in Algeria soon after the end of World War II suggests that only arms were left to compel loyalty.

But there was no gun powerful enough to destroy all the elephants.

2

PIERRE BOURDIEU'S OWN

CULTURAL REVOLUTION

Pierre Bourdieu died in 2002. The following year, among the many tributes to him, was his friends' publication of a small volume of photographs he had taken in Algeria some forty years before, when he was teaching at the University of Algiers. Bourdieu had bought a camera just before he left Europe. He wanted to record scenes from the life of the local population among whom he wished to do ethnographic research. Although well composed, the images in the volume are not very remarkable. And that *is* remarkable: Bourdieu makes no attempt to exoticize or orientalize the subjects of the photos. People are doing everyday things—mostly working—as they would in any other rural or small-town society. There are a few what I call ironies-of-development pictures—a person on a modern motorbike roaring by an old mosque and the like. Algeria constituted this mélange of ways of living in the late 1950s and early 1960s. But so did France. Bourdieu could have returned to his birthplace in a small village in the mountains of the southwest and—allowing for differences of architecture and clothing— made quite similar photos of the mixtures of old and new cultures. In fact, he did return to the Béarn to do investigations very much like those he had done in Algeria. That double move he made in North Africa and then in provincial France lay at the heart of the analytic and cultural revolution he sparked in the empire-freighted social science from which he had to start his own work.

In the years between World Wars I and II, the Paris ethnographic museum held France's largest collection of objects gathered largely from the colonial empire. But one of its halls was dedicated, as well, to the material culture of the French provinces. The shared cult of ethnographic *objects* made for a close connection between the museum and academic ethnologists.[1] In 1937, the French artifacts were separated from the other collections to be given their own museum, the Musée National des Arts et Traditions Populaires (National Museum of Folk Arts and Traditions). This same partition between the ethnographic display of non-European, nonurban, so-called primitive societies and those of the diverse regions of metropolitan France occurred as well in the realm of research. For the land that had championed the universality of humanity, this bifurcation made a sad mistake.[2]

This was the theoretical landscape of the field as Bourdieu entered it in the late 1950s. I will show why these divisions were made, and how, by overcoming them, Bourdieu made a signal theoretical and at the same time political contribution to transcending the negative heritage of colonialism in France. I will divide this account in three parts. First, I will raise some general theoretical considerations about the staking out of different fields of anthropology in the interwar years. I will then discuss what I consider the key turning point in the social sciences, at least in France, in the mid-1930s. Finally, I will assess post-1945 and postcolonial approaches to healing the fissure in the science of humankind, finishing with Pierre Bourdieu's own cultural revolution.

What I want to do is made the more difficult for three reasons. First, the language of the social sciences was in flux during the interwar years. The designations *sociologie, anthropologie, ethnographie, ethnologie,* and *le folklore* were often used interchangeably by writers, and in any case with the greatest imprecision. Second, even when a writer or group gave a precise definition of a discipline, they did not control enough capital in that field to compel the standardization of its language throughout the human sciences. Because the disciplines of society in the 1930s were just becoming at the same time full-fledged sciences and professionalized fields, the definition of their reach and scope generated intense contestation. Marcel Mauss, for example, saw *sociologie,* which mastered best the space of "le tout social," the social totality, as the most general designation for "une science des sociétés," a science of societies.[3] *Ethnologie*, for him and the Durkheimians, made up a subset of the master discipline. On his return from New York after World War II, Claude Lévi-Strauss championed the study of "social anthropology," a label he took from British and American usage; ethnology, to his mind, was subordinate to it. He devoted his own work primarily to overseas societies, leaving to others—primarily Isac Chiva—the care and gatekeeping of the ethnology of metropolitan France.

The final complexity beyond these questions of the internal history of the social sciences is one of understanding their so-called external histories. From the 1920s onward, the social sciences were deeply imbricated with the great political events of the day: colonial rule, the Popular Front, racialist thinking, Vichy, the purging of collaborators after the liberation, and, finally, the postwar repositioning of the sciences of humankind. Knowing the political conjunctures is crucial to understanding the theoretical changes in the social sciences. After World War II, for example, with so much contemporary historical reality pressing in on the scholarly field, many social scientists took a formalist turn—much like their contemporaries in U.S. literary studies turned to the New Criticism—so they might put their houses in order without reality constantly intruding to spoil the symmetry.

Despite the uncertainty and contestation about the definitions of the realms, the project of creating a universal science of humankind initiated during the Enlightenment never quite disappeared in twentieth-century France. Part of this persistence of universalism was, of course, due to the republican ideal inherited from the Great Revolution. But, in addition, with so many leaders of the social sciences from the time of Durkheim to the present first educated as philosophers, French studies of human affairs, although acknowledging the complexity of a real society, have searched for the enduring and the universal. These thinkers officiated as the secular priests of republicanism. With their training in the most prestigious academic discipline of the Third and Fourth Republics, the inventors of the modern social sciences did not shrink back from trying to totalize the sciences of humanity, whether that humanity lived in Africa, the New World, or in provincial France. The creators of the Durkheimian Institut de l'Ethnologie in 1925, for example, remained loyal to this vision of a unified *science de l'Homme* until at least the political and spiritual crises of the interwar years had become unmasterable.

After the romance of the *petit Tonkinois* and the brave *tirailleur Sénégalais* of the immediate post–World War I years—the brief fad for the colonial troops who had fought for the mother country—French colonial policy makers began to turn their backs on the rage for assimilationist policies. With the coming of the economic depression and the growing threat of European war, a great wave of nationalism washed over France.

In parallel fashion, the Indochinese uprisings of 1930 had demonstrated to many colonial officials that the principal source of trouble in the colonies was *déracinement*, the uprooting of local people from their accustomed lives and values. The Paris Colonial Exposition of 1931 tried to foster an ideology of Greater France. But the lessons learned from the almost contemporaneous nationalist and communist uprisings in Indochina pointed the colonial ministry and the military in another direction. The governments of the 1930s systematically began turning to the "chiefs" of real or state-invented "tribes," so valorizing local cultures they earlier had tried, at worst, to destroy or, at best, to ignore. The governments of the Right imposed chief rulers; the Popular Front, when possible, instead promoted leaders who were recognized by the local populations as people of standing. But the new larger project of recognizing and fostering cultural difference remained the same.[4]

Then, in 1935, came a difficult conjunction. In that year the Rockefeller Foundation, until then heavily financing Durkheimian social science, especially research centers like the Sorbonne's Institut de l'Ethnologie, shifted its policy. It announced that in the future it would fund only research on metropolitan France, and only specific projects, rather than, as in the past, annually financing centers of research that in turn ran many diverse investigations both in France and abroad.[5] Writing on behalf of the foundation, the linguist Edward Sapir informed Marcel Mauss that the foundation was no longer interested in funding studies of "the customs and languages of Primitives, and presumably rather useless, people." "To put it more officially," Sapir wrote, "the Rockefeller Foundation has . . . declared its unwillingness to do anything further for anthropology." "It was more important to make people happy," was the justification he gave for the volte-face.[6]

Since it was not a question in the spring of 1935 of the serious and always socially concerned Rockefeller Foundation funding something like a Euro-Disney avant la lettre, the use of the word *happy* seems puzzling. Unless, of course, one considers the socially disruptive effects of the economic depression, the continuing scandal of the Stavisky Affair with the following riots and the police's shooting into a right-wing crowd in Paris on 6–7 February 1934, the astonishing French political turnaround with the signing of a French-Soviet alliance in May 1935, and the unrelieved crisis of the state for the rest of the year as evidence of the pressing need "to make people happy." The colonial ministry, the other major funding source of the institute, continued its support, but it, too, changed its emphasis. It moved the institute's budget lines from those of the various colonies—according to where the research took place—to the central metropolitan office of the ministry. Presumably, this was done better to regulate fulfillment of the Americans' new conditions, that is, in order not to lose the Rockefeller money.

When the Colonial Exposition closed in the fall of 1931, its handsome headquarters building was turned into a permanent Musée des Colonies. The institution was the first such in French history dedicated only to the empire. Recall that since 1886, even the Musée de l'Ethnographie du Trocadéro had had its hall of the regions of France.

When the Popular Front swept into power, Paul Rivet, named in 1928 to head the ethnographic museum, saw his chance to make his own scientific and political statement about the museological representation of the peoples of the world. Originally trained as a navy doctor, Rivet had become a physical anthropologist specializing in Latin American societies. He was, as well, a leading Socialist Party intellectual, even serving for a while as representative in the Chamber for a district of the Latin Quarter.

Rivet and his team remodeled the museum with 1930s hi-tech glass and brass show cases. The halls were uncluttered and remodeled with simple appointments. Michel Leiris, who took part in the repositioning, remembered that they wished to get rid of the look of a trophy room of conquest. The new team intended to have the displays sign the institution as a place where dispassionate scientists studied the material cultures of humankind. In the spirit of the Popular Front, Rivet renamed his refurbished museum the *Musée de l'Homme.*

But an unanticipated consequence of the campaign to unite all French people against the dangers of fascism—into which Rivet threw himself—fostered a kind of national-populist narcissism. For example, in 1937, the French Communist Party (Parti Communiste Français, PCF) held its national congress in Arles, where it celebrated the work of Fréderic Mistral and his society for Provençal renewal, the Félibrige. The word *folklore* was now standardized to refer to the ethnographic study of the French provinces. As Michèle Cointet put it, "Art for the people [both Left and Right agreed] would once again find its roots in folklore."[7] The Right and the Left did battle—in the streets as much as on the printed page—over who would speak for the *pays réel* (for the true country, as against the one for the moment in power). This new passionate struggle over the meaning of the nation's popular traditions encouraged the study and celebration of folklore, even including briefly, in the years of the Popular Front, workers' folklore.

Yet this seemingly grand moment for the science of popular culture must be punctuated with a question mark. Rivet divided the hall of France from the rest of the museum and gave it separate status as the national museum of French popular culture. He meant thereby to contribute to this new celebration of the *populaire* in France. However, at the same time, the creation of the Musée National des Arts et Traditions Populaires put into question both institutionally and *in theory* the universalist premise grounding the study of humankind. Rivet wanted to make a political statement about the "defense of culture" against the new German barbarism; he wanted the new museum of popular culture opened as soon as possible, ideally for the 1937 Exposition Internationale. But the new hall of French folk culture was not ready in time. In fact it remained closed to the public from the collapse of the Popular Front, to the advent of Marshal Pétain's new regime, and through the war years.[8]

Rivet put at the head of the Musée National des Arts et Traditions Populaires a man of great talent, but by no means a museum specialist. Georges-Henri Rivière turned out to be a genius of museology. His biographer entitled her book about him *The Magician of the Display*

Case. But without higher degrees or formal museum training, he was a genius that Rivet could control. Rivet's departure for Latin America with the Gestapo on his heals suddenly gave Rivière unexpected freedom of action. Rivière used the opportunity to expand prewar investigations of architecture and domestic furnishings in the French provinces.[9]

Despite splendid exhibitions of regional architecture that the new museum had sponsored already at the exposition of 1937, and the rural field work in the Vichy years, the Musée National des Arts et Traditions Populaires itself remained closed to the public until after the Liberation. That meant that, unhindered by any accessible alternative vision, a fascistic representation of the regional and popular cultures of France could be projected in the massive peasantist propaganda of the revolutionary conservatives around Marshal Philippe Pétain. We are fortunate to have Christian Faure's *Le projet culturel de Vichy* on this sad period. Faure has demonstrated how elaborate indeed was this reprovincializing of France under the marshal.[10]

Although l'État Français, that is, the French government in Vichy, and the Other France in London and Africa both worked to keep the colonial empire out of German hands in the years of the war, little ethnological research work in France d'Outre-Mer was possible. But, as much as possible, colonial politics carried on. Eric Jennings's *Vichy in the Tropics* has shown that the Vichy authorities in many parts of the French Empire encouraged the same Pétainist values of local cultures, as well as empowering old local elites to enforce them.[11] In fact, it continued the same policies Faure described in the case of the provinces. Such ideologically driven regional-colonial policies did not see any value in following the practices of republican social sciences.

The Vichy officials felt certain that in every French person's heart was a "true France" of the provinces. Accordingly, they endorsed a "true Indochina" for the Asian colonials, a "true Madagascar," a "true New Caledonia," and so forth. These essential identities had always existed, they had just to be freed from past republican constrictions and overlays. Of course, not a trivial reason for this universalism of localisms was the intensified regionalization forced on France by the German occupation. Then, too, there was the fear of Vichy (and Gaullist authorities) that the peoples of the empire might believe the anticolonial promises of nationalist agitators, or the blandishments of the Japanese

Co-prosperity Sphere. This period in the history of the sciences and social sciences both of metropolitan and overseas France is ripe for further exploration.

Some ethnographic research, as I said, was possible in the metropole during the occupation. Rivière organized his investigations as the Chantiers Intellectuels (Intellectual Worksites). The Nazi occupiers saw no dangers in studies of the material culture of provincial France that his teams pilled up. The Chantiers Intellectuels were for museology what Marcel Carné's *Les enfants du paradis*, made in 1944 in occupied Paris, was for the film industry, a big project with many participants to evade the Service de Travail Obligatoire, the labor draft for work in Germany. But like *les films français de qualité* (French films of quality) made under the German occupation, and recently honored in Bertrand Tavernier's *Laisser-Passez* (2000), many unresolved ambiguities about the behavior of the French participants remain still to discuss. The researchers in the projects of the Musée National des Arts et Traditions Populaires, like the filmmakers mostly decent people trying to survive, had to make compromises inevitably burdening them in different degrees of culpability to hold out in a bad situation. But during those Vichy years, the French folklorist focus which paralleled Nazi interest in the rural German *Volk* seriously compromised the discipline of folklore in France. Hence the need for that name and its practices to disappear after the Liberation.[12]

So we see here one of those ironies that makes history so fascinating and so difficult at the same time. The attempt to honor popular France, at the moment of the Popular Front, had the unintended consequences of formally dividing the history of the peoples in different parts of the world imbricated in the history of France. Now toward some promising solutions.

After the war and the Vichy episode, several serious attempts were made beginning in the 1950s and 1960s to end the epistemological schism that had marked off two divergent sciences of humankind for but one humanity. First, of course, after the racism of Vichy and the mobilization of the discipline of folklore to construct the ruralist fantasies of Marshal Pétain and the romantic fascists in his circle, Lévi-Strauss's postwar writings against race-thinking and racism proved very important. He of course demonstrated that race was neither a scientific nor a useful social category. But even more, he rejected Lucien Lévy-Bruhl's idea of a primitive *mentalité* (mind set) that differed from the *mentalité* of Europeans. By means of his universalized structuralist conception of mythic thought, Lévi-Strauss reestablished, philosophically—so very abstractly to be sure—a universal ideal of humankind: we all think the same, if differently. But even the different myths we live by resemble each other structurally. Remember, too, that his important first book dealt with kinship. The study of kinship takes account of ethnic differences, but it does not make value judgments about them. Everyone in the world, after all, lives within a kinship system. None is better or worse than another.

Then there was the less well-known contemporary work of Georges Balandier. His vision of a discipline, which he usually called "sociology," that looked at what he termed the "colonial situation" linked the interactive actions, thoughts, and questions of both the metropole and the colonies into a potentially powerful universal social science. Theoretically, he did not fully work out his concept of the colonial situation; only today are younger scholars, most notably Emmanuelle Saada, developing this fruitful strategy for ending the great schism of humanity cut by the French social scientists.[13]

As an American, I should not forget to mention the work in the past several decades of Immanuel Wallerstein and his coworkers at the Fernand Braudel Center. Starting from the promising premise that there can be only one dominant mode of production in the modern world, Wallerstein fashioned a complex historical sociology of the capitalist world system. His early analyses were weakened, I think, by his refusal to integrate culture into his strictly materialist paradigm. But it must be noted that he became one of the first specialists on African *sociology*—his preferred name for his discipline—to theorize what we today call globalization.[14]

Now finally, we come to how Pierre Bourdieu pointed the way out of the postcolonial crisis of the social sciences. In an important interview with Pierre Lamaison in *Terrains* in 1985—where Bourdieu explains his move "from rules to strategies" (de la règle aux stratégies), he judged that "there is something perverse about the existence of ethnology as a separate science." For "while seeming to respect" the colonial societies it studies, as well as, more recently, European peasants and even workers, it continues "to create an unbridgeable gap [between Europeans and primitives], as in the good old days when people still spoke of a 'primitive mind.'"[15] Later looking back to his earliest key articles on, first, the Kaybles of Algeria, then, his using the same methods to study his compatriots of his native Béarn in the Pyrenees, and, finally, his later studies of the tribe of Paris intellectuals, he characterizes his grand project, "for twenty years now, all my work has aimed at abolishing this fissure [*l'opposition*] between ethnology and sociology."[16]

Note first the pattern of his early writings. He began doing anthropology while he taught at the University of Algers, after his military service during the war of independence from the French. Then, when he returned home, he did a number of articles on the family strategies of the peasants of his native Béarn.[17] His earliest work in the ethnology of the Berbers and of Algeria was initially influenced by the work of Lévi-Strauss. The specialist on European ethnology, Isac Chiva, who worked closely with Lévi-Strauss at the Laboratory of Social Anthropology, helped him publish one of his earliest articles. But then Bourdieu began to rethink the categories of kinship (*parenté*) that Lévi-Strauss had elaborated in the book he had written during the war in the New York Public Library.

A powerful new idea came to him while doing fieldwork at home. As a proper disciple of Lévi-Strauss, Bourdieu traced the kinship relations acknowledged by his former neighbors in southwestern France. He dutifully charted what local people told him were kinship patterns of their village. But then he discovered a curious anomaly. He kept finding that the community rules that people told him reigned—for example, for who could or could not marry whom, who inherited, who was seen as a relative—so clearly and neatly marked in the kinship charts local informants helped him make—seemed not at all to describe what people in fact *did*. There were exceptions.

But there are always exceptions in social research. Social sciences deal with people, after all, not atomic particles. Most social scientists seeking to discover laws of human behavior make peace with such untidiness. Relatively high statistical covariation is all one can hope for in investigative social science, or so holds the norm. But Bourdieu had the genius to meditate on the numerous violations of what everyone he asked called the rules. He began to consider a possible new line of thinking in which the exceptions, not the rules, made the society.

Now in the early 1960s, Bourdieu began to develop his decisive methodological switch from investigating the sociological *laws* of kinship to observing the *strategies* of families and groups. He became increasingly engrossed now with how families and groups manipulated the social rules that, all agreed, at the same time remained normative. And as he applied his new questions and methods to the Kaybles, his compatriots in the villages of the Béarn, and to the warring clans of Parisian intellectuals, a new kind of universalizable—if not law-driven—social science began to take form.

Clearly he was attempting a theoretical move that would allow him to treat the situation of the Berbers in the mountains of Algeria and his own hometown in the Pyrenees without cramming all into a totalized system. On his return to Paris from Algeria he had suggested to Raymond Aron, his thesis director and also a philosopher who had made himself into a social scientist, that he, Bourdieu, do his thesis on the Berbers in Algeria. Aron would not hear of it. "It is a subject unworthy of you," he told the brilliant young graduate of the elite École Normale Supérieure. Bourdieu was stubborn: he wrote the study, but not as a doctoral thesis; he never did one.[18]

By 1974, he had begun systematically to draw the research implications of his theoretical insight. As he said in his final comments to an important conference of his team held in 1974 at Jussieu,

> We have to exhume all that [the colonial experience], explain it, because that is to do the socio-analysis of our collective understanding, of the apparatus of thought with which we think both consciously and unconsciously. Everything that I will now say about colonial sociology can equally be said about the sociology of French society. It would be fascinating systematically to analyze the systems of thought used to think the peasants and the working class in France and the systems of thought employed for thinking the Algerians. For example, is it only accidental that the first institutions to teach agriculture called themselves "colonies"; is it just by chance that the colonial metaphor is always present in the history of education?[19]

In rejecting the inherited theoretical distance between a poor province of France and the Algerian Kaybles, Bourdieu at the same time also rejected the sociopolitical gap. Taught first by village school teachers, sent on to study in the lycée in nearby Pau, then to Paris for the high-level cram courses given in the famous lycées there to prepare for the exams to enter the Grandes Écoles, and finally accepted to the École Normale Supérieure—where he graduated first in his class—Bourdieu disliked centrifugal social movements. He was a classic child of the Republic; he looked for unifying visions. In practice that meant he studied the unjust barriers raised by origins, education, culture, and colonial status separating members of what he deeply believed was a common humanity.[20] His strongly felt refusal to ontologize difference went so deep that at one point in Pierre Carles's film about him, *La sociologie est un sport de combat* (2001), he admits that when he hears the distinctive accent of his native Béarn it puts his teeth on edge. He had taught himself to speak with no such accent. At the height of the regionalist protest movements of the 1970s, he wrote negatively, even disparagingly, of them. He did not think that the word *"region"* made for a useful scientific designation.[21]

Pierre Bourdieu's deconstruction of the scientific and political boundaries between ethnology and sociology made a decisive move to address the European crisis of postcoloniality. Bourdieu found his own way out of the crisis following decolonization, not by putting forth a social science of universal laws, but rather by working out a universal *method of work*. In the last decade of his life, he was criticized for having abandoned serious social science to devote himself to political pamphleteering and journalism. Yet I am convinced that, from the start, Bourdieu's work was informed in equal parts by rigorous science and a deep commitment to bettering the condition of the oppressed.[22] With the death of this man who considered sociology a martial art, *un sport de combat*, we have lost a brilliant fighter for social justice.

3

JEAN RENOIR'S VOYAGE OF DISCOVERY

From the Shores of the Mediterranean to

the Banks of the Ganges

For reasons both social and artistic, aesthetic modernism has drawn a line between art and society. I think more fruitful for enriching our knowledge of both art and our world is Stephen Greenblatt's argument that "the work of art is the product of a negotiation between a creator, or class of creators, equipped with a complex, communally shared repertoire of conventions, and the institutions and practices of society."[1] For such a project, the political films of Jean Renoir—from *Toni* to *The River*, from 1934 to 1951—are good to think with. But neither of these were political films in the sense of his *La vie est à nous* (Our life belongs to us, 1936) or *La Marseillaise* (The Marseillaise, 1938). By following the arc of the films from the 1930s to the 1950s, we will see that *Toni* and *The River* are political in an important international way—a culturally *global* way—as the films made during the Popular Front are not.

We may gain a good sense of the making of politics and art in the two decades before the era of decolonization by tracking the traffic between contemporary political life, political history, and the sphere of aesthetic representation in the cinema. Following Renoir's changing self-positioning in the Franco-French civil war, and finally his declaring himself a noncombatant, will open for us a key perspective for situating Renoir in the making of prewar and postwar France.[2] He made his three important nationalist, or better to say, "True France," films—*La vie est à nous*, *La Marseillaise*, and *La règle du jeu* (The rules of the game, 1939)—in the intensely politically agitated years of the Popular Front. *Toni*, his sympathetic film about the hard lives of some immigrant workers in the South of France, he made at the start of the French depression. And *The River*, an American production he made in India, dates from just four years after that nation gained independence, although it has nothing to do with that theme; it opts out of any world beyond that of daily life and troubled loves.

In what follows, I want to be a *Grenzgänger*, to contribute to the project of crossing the guarded borders between cultural production and politics.[3] In terms of the project of this book—to trace how empire subverts democracy—Renoir's itinerary from a local community on the Mediterranean, to the nation being remade on the Seine, and, finally, to the tranquility of the slowly moving river of life in India will prove instructive. Accordingly, let us first look at the apparently apolitical *Toni* to see Renoir's deep sense of inclusiveness at its most humanist expression.[4] Just two years later, a government of a newly united Left formed to resist the manifestations of Italian and German fascism at home. Renoir put his full creative energies to supporting the Popular Front. His commitment makes for the immediate context and raison d'être of Renoir's three political films I will discuss. And then, finally, we will consider rest and peace in an eternal Asia.

There is, in addition, the question of what makes left art. Here, we can situate the films within what Peter Bürger and Christa Bürger have called the "institution of art,"[5] meaning in the first instance not the sociological or operational structures of art funding, the recruitment of actors, film technology, and so on, but, rather, the set of basic assumptions and norms in a given historical context that validate particular aesthetic practices and marginalize others. France's heady experience of the Popular Front framed aesthetic expression—the institution of art— when Renoir was making his political films. In his chapter on Renoir, Dudley Andrew in fact calls him "a kind of institution set within the larger institution of the film industry . . . a source and a resource."[6]

Specifically, the dominant institution of art in the French films of the 1930s was aesthetic realism (sometimes called poetic realism), which guided French filmmaking and overshadowed, or, more precisely, made it virtually impossible to theorize, available expressionist or surrealist options. We can learn something about the political and aesthetic context of French *cinéma engagé* (politically committed film), and perhaps sound some problems of political art, in the intersections of these several Boolean rings of signification. And, most important and yet agreeable, we can follow the war over French identity, and Renoir's moves and movies, from the plush seats of a French cinema.

PLAYING THE MARSEILLAISE AND
THE INTERNATIONAL IN HARMONY

In the years before the rise to power in Germany of the National Socialists and Adolf Hitler, the Comintern had encouraged its member parties to pursue a go-it-alone, class-against-class strategy in domestic politics. So in Germany, the KPD (Kommunistische Partei Deutschlands), refusing any coalitions, infamously denounced the Social Democrats as "social fascists" and encouraged things to get worse so that the better might be born. Hoping to win the disaffected to their ranks, they rejected collaboration with the other labor party and other nonfascist groups in a Germany where Socialist and Communist votes, if united, could have made both popular and parliamentary majorities. Hitler's coming to power in January 1933, and the Nazi consolidation of rule in 1934, forced the Comintern and leaders of the parties of the Second International who had played their own big part in poisoning the political culture of the Left, to rethink their strategies. In particular in France, with spontaneous workers' gestures of amity across party lines setting the direction, the national political mood swung around 180 degrees. The new defensive strategy called for uniting all antifascist and simply nonfascist political forces in defense of democracy against dictatorship, humanism against racism and imperialism, culture against barbarism, France against Germany.

Initiated in 1934, after violent right-wing demonstrations (usually referred to as the Stavisky riots) appeared to many on the Left as an attempt to topple the republican government, and formally promulgated in 1935, France's first Popular Front government arrived in power in June 1936. The coalition won the elections in May. But even before the new ministers took up their portfolios, widespread strikes and the workers' greater expectations of rapid improvement of their lot—after finally having elected their government—created a national mood of political urgency. Racing to keep up with their rank and file, the new Popular Front government immediately initiated an unprecedented program of social reform: the forty-hour week, four weeks of paid vacation, the nationalization of the central bank and of the armaments industry, and compulsory arbitration of labor disputes.

In order to understand the politics of *La vie est à nous* and *La Marseillaise*, and indeed of *La règle du jeu* as well, it is important to keep in mind that the Parti Communiste Français (PCF) supported the government of Léon Blum in the Chamber, but discreetly refused to take any cabinet portfolios so as not to frighten more moderate alliance partners. Perhaps, too, it did not want to offend its own left wing. And, of course, the party wished to retain its freedom of action both in politics and in economic contests involving its ally, the Confédération Générale du Travail, the major trade union confederation. But just because it did not form part of the government, the PCF could influence events only by bargaining with its votes and steering public opinion to pressure the government from the left, or more accurately, to reduce right-wing pressures on it. With no ministerial power, but a friendly government, the PCF actively pursued two parallel policies: the first was to maximize its representatives in a parliament it had scorned only a few years before, and, accordingly, to convince its militants that at this juncture in history, votes made for the best weapons of the working class. The second, in collaboration with Socialists and bourgeois radicals, was to launch a media campaign in defense of culture against the Right. This was the culture of the Enlightenment and its heirs, to be sure, not the *Kultur* claiming to embody the uniqueness of German identity. So, commissioning one of France's great directors to make an electoral film like *La vie est à nous*—shown to members and supporters at meetings and private showings, rather than in ordinary commercial cinemas—on the eve of the parliamentary elections of 1936 made good sense. Militants had to be assured that an armistice had been negotiated in the class war waged so rigorously by the party in the preceding Third Period.

Intersecting the sphere of practical politics was the struggle over who spoke for the France of the day, and, much the same question during the period, who spoke for historic France. Parallel to the other parties of the Third International, the PCF played the card of nationalism: all classes together in the defense of the nation. As the head of the party, Maurice Thorez put the issue in his report to the Seventh Party Congress in December 1937: the PCF had to address the pressing need to forge the "Unity of the French Nation." "By reviving the noblest national and revolutionary traditions of our people, the French Communist Party reconciled the red flag and the tricolor, the *Marseillaise* and the *Internationale.*"[7] Thorez was proposing the reconciliation of all but the most resolute combatants in the Franco-French civil war by asking all to embrace both social justice and the nation. Renoir's *La Marseillaise* shows the same union in defense of a revolutionary nation formed in the heat of the struggles against internal and external enemies.[8]

TONI

The party's and Renoir's emphasis on the true nation was new, at least for the latter. *Toni*, the 1934 film Renoir made in his new realist style, although about foreigners, had not at all raised the question of who belonged in France and who did not. Or better said, it empathized with the thousands of immigrant workers who had come to France to replace the 1.4 million dead of the Great War, and who now, with a shortage of jobs because of the depression, had begun to be resented by some of the "true" French.

Toni tells the story of labor and love among an ethnically and nationally diverse group of workers employed in a quarry in Martigues, Provence. The foreign workers—Italians, Spaniards—mix easily with the Corsican and Midi peasant laborers. One of the quarry workers is played by an African American Renoir found working in Martigues when he started shooting. Although the actors speak French with strong accents and the film was made completely on location, Renoir avoids the cuteness of language, character, and custom with which Marcel Pagnol decorates his stories and films of the Midi.[9] Nor is the character played by the black man, the guitar player, at all thematized as *black;* he is just another one of the poor workers.

In a kind of filmed *faits divers*, Toni and Josefa, both foreigners, love each other. But the (French) foreman of the quarry, Albert, encounters Josefa alone and rapes her in a ditch. Toni mistakenly believes she succumbed willingly and, in disgust, rejects her. Pregnant from the assault, Josefa feels there is no choice but to marry her attacker. In despair Toni enters a loveless union with another woman. But after all, Toni still loves Josefa and she him. Finally, one day, defending herself against the frequently abusive behavior of her husband, Josefa picks up his gun and shoots him dead. Toni arrives at the house soon after and tries to hide her crime. When the lovers are found out by the police, Toni is shot while trying to run away. A love tragedy of poor immigrant workers speaking with strong accents played by unknown local actors: Renoir said that he wanted to shoot the film so that, unsuspected by the characters, the people in the audience might feel that they are actually watching these lives unfold.[10]

As Jonathan Buchsbaum has written, "*Toni* presents one community in France as an immigrant culture, cris-crossed by languages and customs, yet with no discourse of authenticity or nation." Dudley Andrew calls the film's Zola-esque style "documentary realism."[11] It confronted the viewer with an unhappy reality; the film failed badly at the box office. During the depression, Pagnol's jolly French survivors in the Midi were what the public wanted to see, not suffering foreigners.

Whereas *Toni* radiates the kind of grassroots universal humanism that Renoir so cherished, *La Marseillaise* confronts the—for Renoir—totally new question of who are the true French and who are not. And being one of the true French, at least in Renoir's story, was important for a person's survival during the French Revolution.

A SONG OF LOVE

The photographer Lotte Eisner reports a conversation in which Renoir described the opening he considered for a new historical film. At first, viewers were to observe two peasants fishing along a river, perhaps the Seine or a tributary. A body floats by; then another one. After seeing several more dead people, one peasant was to turn to the other and say, "Jean, I think there's something going on in Paris."[12]

But Renoir did not start the film with naive provincials far from the center of power guessing at the meaning of great events from gruesome clues, even if the scene would have clearly announced the film as a history of great events viewed from below, the way simpler people—among whom the filmmaker counted himself—might experience the world. After some thought, Renoir probably realized that his contemplated opening had an inadvertent sick-joke quality about it. More important, to begin with the results of bloodshed in faraway Paris would have misdirected the viewer's eye for a film in which Renoir wished to represent the Revolution as a rare moment of social reconciliation, national unity, and emotional solidarity in France.

Instead, he chose to begin *La Marseillaise* with an establishing shot showing the king amid his court in its splendor, as one would begin a history from above. Yet we see a court so grand, courtiers so different from other mortals—so separated from ordinary people—that Renoir nevertheless forces the viewer to see from below by overwhelming us with this small claustrophobic world. It was too splendid, too rich, too cut off from the people of 1789, and, in his vision, alienated from *the same people* in 1937. In the late 1930s, France suffered deep economic depression; the distance ordinary people felt between themselves and the glorious royal court on the screen could not have been greater. Here Renoir achieved his friend Bertolt Brecht's alienation effect by making scenes too large for life. Even though he began his film within the palace, Renoir brilliantly carried off his representation of the French Revolution from the point of view of those in the streets, called in eighteenth-century France "the little people." It was these little people and their descendants who Renoir celebrated at different moments in both *La vie est à nous* and *La Marseillaise*. In the mid-1930s Renoir felt that the PCF and the Confédération Générale du Travail best represented the people of France against those who ignored or scorned and oppressed them.

Interviewed by Jean Kress in the communist youth magazine *L'Avant-Garde* soon after he had completed *La Marseillaise*, Renoir explained his choice of theme:

In view of all the productions having nothing whatsoever to do with France as it really is today [*la France actuelle*], alas, the great majority of what is made, my friends and I have sensed, for some time now, the necessity of making a film representing the little people of France [*la France populaire*]. The best subject, clearly, would have been what is happening today: the May victory [of the Popular Front in the elections], the strikes in June. . . . It would have been magnificent, but the film would never have been distributed. So, we switched to the epoch that most resembled our own: the French Revolution.[13]

The years between 1787 and 1815, from the calling of the Estates-General by the bankrupt monarchy to the final defeat of Napoleon and the restoration of the Bourbons, are usually counted as the revolutionary era. The period contains a rich archive for aesthetic invention to draw on. By choosing the year 1792—before the execution of the king and queen, before the Jacobin dictatorship and the Terror, before the blatant corruption of the Directory, and before Napoleon's dictatorship and perversion of the Revolution—Renoir could make a film about brotherhood (*fraternité*).

This last value of the republican trinity had proven the most difficult to define, let alone make public practice. Freedom (*liberté*) could be conquered; equality (*égalité*) could be measured and fought for in income distribution, access to schooling, and social mobility. But Renoir was championing the political virtue of social solidarity, something that republican and later Socialist governments to this day have had difficulty in realizing. Humanity as one, ties of loyalty and affection, universal friendship—these were the deep values that informed Renoir's films in this period and, I would suggest, throughout his career.

Each time we see *La Marseillaise*, Renoir's humanity both moves and amazes us: a song with rather bloodthirsty lyrics, written during a Revolution that divided and continues today to divide the people of France, serves as the protagonist of a film that celebrates the largely peaceful unity of the French people. Against this unity we are shown only a tiny domestic enemy, but very powerful foreign ones. From the film's beginning, showing patriots in faraway Marseilles forming a regiment to aid their Parisian brothers in defending the Revolution, to the last scene of the united soldiers of the Revolution marching to do battle with the invading Prussians at Valmy, the unity of the French people— which would overcome internal divisions *and* growing foreign (German) dangers—suffused the action. The scene he did not film, of bodies floating in the river, would have clashed mightily with his final vision of the meaning of the French upheaval. In *La Marseillaise*, as Renoir put it in his memoirs, he offered his personal reading of the theme of national unity: "For a short time the French really believed that they could love one another. We felt ourselves borne on a wave of goodwill."[14]

The we of the film was as inclusive as Renoir's vision of the Popular Front. It included Arnaud, the articulate petit bourgeois with some education (a kind of eighteenth-century political commissar of the Marseilles regiment); Bomier, the mason (the building trades functioned as strongholds of the Communist Party in the 1930s); the painter, a bit like Jean-Louis David, standing for the arts; peasant supporters waving to the troops as they passed—the little people of France all united by culture, by a song written by someone with an aristocratic-sounding *de* in his name and brought from Strasbourg by, the script takes care to have a character note, a Jewish peddler. (Recall that the premier of the government of unity was Léon Blum, a fact that injected anti-Semitic venom to the Right's vicious political campaign against it.) In the film we also see the irresolute Alsatian soldiers in the Tuileries Palace, addressed by one of the charging patriots in their local patois, finally refusing to defend the monarchy against the armed nation. Renoir's sense of the unity of the French people and of French (high) culture extended even to the exiled nobility, portrayed with surprising warmth in the film. However, separated from the nation, they had begun to forget the steps to the court dances; they were losing their very Frenchness. By turning against the French people and fleeing into exile, the émigrés who left France for Coblenz to await the overthrow of the people's will were losing touch with the civilization of France. By contrast, we see foreigners—Marie-Antoinette, aristocrats with German names in court, and the Swiss Guards—as enemies of the nation. They alone are presented coldly, as strangers to the communion of the French people.

This conception of the social forces arrayed in the Revolution corresponds to the prevailing left interpretation of the Revolution taught in the schools in the mid-1930s, which facilitated this theme of unity, if only in the negative sense of the many forces arrayed against the old political order. The professor of the history of the French Revolution at the Sorbonne, Georges Lefèbvre, himself a member of the PCF, spoke and wrote of three overlapping revolutions: first, the aristocrats' rebellion against the king's attempt to get them to support financially the bankrupt state, which started the questioning of royal authority even before 1789; second, the peasants' uprising and seizure of the lands of the church and the nobles; and third—the radical high point—the urban revolution of the Jacobins. Thus, in this understanding of the course of the Revolution, most of the French wanted radical change. The bankruptcy of the ancien régime was clearly more than just fiscal; its reversal was not the main problem. Foreign enemies within and without continued to thwart the general will of the people of France.[15]

THE BOLSHEVIKS OF 1792

When the Russian Left tried to understand the course of the 1917 Revolution in Russia to assess their options and the possible outcomes, they studied what most Socialists understood as its precursor in France. In Leon Trotsky's accounts, for example, the Stalinist distortion of the 1917 Revolution is compared to Napoleon's betrayal of his Jacobin origins. So Thorez's citation of Lenin's frequently repeated formula, "The Bolsheviks are the Jacobins of the proletarian revolution," was received by the assembled delegates at the party congress in Arles as the statement of a self-evident historical parallel.[16] In the interwar years, the science of historical materialism guaranteed that the similarities between the two events were linked by well-established laws of social development. But this pairing of the two revolutions suggests a more conflictual and certainly bloodier version of radical social transformation than Renoir's own take, the unity of all French patriots against a tiny minority (in the film, literally a roomful) of aristocrats and a small group of stupid (the Swiss Guard) or evil (the queen and her circle) foreigners.

The idea of the Great Revolution captured in the Lenin-Thorez metaphor, that the one in 1789 constituted a kind of rehearsal, or first try, for that of 1917—not Renoir's special vision of national unity—prevailed in French history writing until French intellectuals turned on the PCF after the invasion first of Hungary in 1956, and in greater numbers after the Soviet tanks rolled into Prague in 1968. The student uprising of May 1968 completed the disenchantment with Communism. Thereafter, in the 1970s, led by the historian and former party member François Furet, the old Marxist conception of the Revolution came under heavy attack. Furet and his followers argued that post-1917 understandings of the French Revolution actually enacted readings of the Russian Revolution back to the future; rather than the Bolsheviks looking to the French Revolution for guidance, twentieth-century communist history writing had rewritten the story to make the Jacobins the Bolsheviks of the French Revolution.[17] The Furet critique, which, more than a quarter century later, continues to loom powerfully over current discussions, sees the classic Marxist narrative of the French Revolution as a kind of justificatory mythic pedigree for the Bolshevik Revolution, to be sure. But on this Jaurèsean-Marxist account the PCF had also built its claim for the centrality of the PCF in French life: it acted, after all, as the keeper and embodiment of the republic's founding myth.

Yet with the decline of the French Communist Party in the course of the 1970s, Furet returned to a vision similar to Renoir's in *La Marseillaise*. In the first chapter of his 1978 book, Furet declared the French Revolution at an end. He meant that the Leninist linkage of 1789 and 1917 had finally broken down. But he also suggested in the book that the Revolution no longer marked the point of fissure of France's contending political communities, that, finally, a national consensus had emerged which accepted the values and results of 1789. But like Daniel Bell's famous *End of Ideology*, published in 1960, Furet's rush to historical closure proved premature. For, to mark the 1989 bicentennial, the governing Socialists, in the tradition of the 1889 centennial, which had positioned the new Third Republic as the direct heir of 1789, tried to present the course of French history as a prelude to their electoral victory.[18] Their attempt to take control of the myth of the Revolution met with some success, although their ceremonies—especially their postmodern parade on 14 July—were greeted either by bad reviews, charges of politicizing this part of the national heritage, or, worst of all, by public indifference. Even today, racist exclusionists like Jean-Marie Le Pen can gain enough organizational and electoral support for his anti-immigrant campaign to preclude as premature any celebration of the triumph of the French Revolution's ideal of *fraternité*.

WHOSE CULTURE?

I want now to explore the French mythology of national unity in its specifically aesthetic manifestation. To begin, let me quote for a last time from Thorez's 1937 "Report to the 1937 Party Congress," for culture assumes an important place in Thorez's speech. Noting the greater participation of French workers in French culture, he proudly reported an increase of workers' visits to the Louvre, Versailles, the Arc de Triomphe, and the Panthéon. Turning to cinema, again in the idiom of the Russian five-year plans, he emphasized that French film production was up. Moreover,

> Three French films won the highest awards at the International Biennial of Venice. Among these films are *La grande illusion* by our dear friend Jean Renoir (applause) who gave our Party *La vie est à nous* and who is now completing *La Marseillaise*. Our comrade Dreyfus gave us *Le temps des cerises*. How much honest and sincere effort in order to give our people a cinema powerful in its conception and interpretation, striking because of its emphasis on the truth, and the collective acting and quality of the artists, both the great stars and the supporting casts.[19]

I cite Thorez's aesthetic appreciations here to allow us entry into the creative context—the hegemonic institution of art during the period of our films.

On Friday, 21 June 1935 in the grand auditorium of the Mutualité on the Left Bank in Paris, André Gide convened a meeting of many of the West's greatest writers: "Literature has never been more alive. Never has so much been written and printed in France and in all civilized countries. Why then do we keep hearing that our culture is in danger?"[20] With this challenging question he opened the first International Congress of Writers for the Defense of Culture. Clearly, in 1935 the trope of defending culture referred back to the Great War and the defense of the values of the West against the German invaders, who had fought for their own, non-Western *Kultur*. Equally clearly, the contemporary danger to culture came once again from Germany. Hitler and the National Socialists had been ruling in Berlin for two years; they had crushed the Left, burned books, and had begun to rearm Germany.

Making culture the issue to unite antifascist forces allowed many noncommunist writers to participate without fearing that they might be used or sensing themselves in a condition of *mauvaise foi*, bad faith. French Culture—*civilisation* in the face of fascist *barbarie*—united all French, including workers, or so the Left's stratagem went, at a fiercely fought moment of the longterm Franco-French civil war. Among French writers, Gide's presiding role at the conference made him most prominent, but participating in important ways were also, among others, André Malraux, Louis Aragon, Paul Éluard, Paul Nizan, Jean Cassou, André Chamson, Jean-Richard Bloch, Jean Guéhenno, and Julien Benda. Jules Romains, Henri de Montherlant, and Georges Duhamel had been invited but had not accepted. Naturally, writers of the far Right, such as Louis-Ferdinand Céline, were not wanted; nor were those perceived as frivolous, such as Jean Cocteau.

The names of the foreign writers asked to participate, and accepted, offer us a dazzling display of the literary culture of the West in the interwar years. Although neither Thomas Mann nor George Bernard Shaw could attend, they agreed to have their names inscribed as members of the congress's presidium. From England came E. M. Forster and Aldous Huxley. German exiled writers attended in great numbers, including Bertolt Brecht, Johannes Becher, Lion Feuchtwanger, Anna Seghers, and Heinrich Mann. The Russians included Isaac Babel, Ilya Ehrenburg, Boris Pasternak, and Alexei Tolstoi. Mike Gold and Waldo Frank represented American left letters.

That the defense of culture should be first mounted in Paris was by 1935 one of those things that went without saying among intellectuals both in France and the rest of nonfascist Europe. In April of the same year, a Communist-organized First American Writers' Congress had preceded the one in Paris and in February 1936 the First American Artists' Congress convened in New York. As is evident from the designation *American*, the organizers and participants of these meetings made no claims to speak for the West. Roger Shattuck's otherwise informative essay on the Paris congress errs, I think, in one judgment: his assertion that "in the mid-thirties, France had assumed cultural leadership of Europe by default."[21] The cultural leadership of Europe had for centuries been a part of French leaders' sense of national destiny. That these particular conference leaders were largely Communists makes little difference; they were *French* Communists, and other European intellectuals, Communists and non-Communists alike, readily endorsed the cultural leadership of their land. What was this endangered French culture? What did it mean for workers?

Jacques Soustelle, in 1936–37 a young anthropologist and a Socialist, characterized the cultural project of the Popular Front as one that would "open the gates of culture and break down the barriers which, like [the iron fence of] a beautiful park forbidden to the poor, enclose a culture reserved for a privileged elite." The goal of giving access to *the* culture was set largely by the Communists, but their alliance partners shared it. No one, at least no one in office or in the PCF, contemplated fostering new modes of creation. As Julian Jackson has pointed out, the Popular Front aimed at "the democratization of an existing traditional culture."[22] Pascal Ory, author of our best study of the cultural politics of the period, describes the agenda as a demand on the bourgeoisie to give workers back their heritage (*patrimoine*).[23] *Regards*, the PCF picture magazine, speaking of the culture as if it made up a part of surplus value, urged workers to "take back what was stolen from us."

For his part, Renoir wished to take back the Revolution from the great figures and give it back to the little people who made it. In keeping with Renoir's take on the French Revolution, but out of keeping with the usual narrative, only one of the famous revolutionary leaders of the textbooks is named in the film. To locate the ideological horizon of the Marseilles volunteers, and of the filmmaker, Renoir has Arnaud inquire after Robespierre when the southerners arrive in Paris. These militant provincials march into a highly contested political arena: Girondists, Jacobins, early anarchists, revolutionary feminists, opportunists, and, of course, traitors. From this short passage we learn that Renoir, the film, and the soldiers from Marseilles supported the Jacobin republic, which according to PCF historiography marked both the high point and political limit of the Revolution. Arnaud's asking after Robespierre drew the political horizon of the film and, for the PCF and its supporters, conferred its imprimatur.[24]

That the PCF preferred certain political content in cultural products should come as no surprise, though its conservatism about the forms of the culture it endorsed in the 1930s seems at the same time glaring and puzzling.[25] That such a posture was not inevitable, the universal result of the dead hand of Zhdanovist aesthetics, may be seen by recalling the rich debates within Weimar Germany's Left, notably between Georg Lukács's advocacy of realism as the supreme art form recognized by Socialist criticism (with Walter Scott, Honoré de Balzac, and Thomas Mann as its heroes) and Walter Benjamin's support of the Brechtian epic theater in Germany and of surrealism in France.[26] Renoir and Brecht were friends, and we may guess that the scenes of speakers addressing the movie audience directly in *La vie est à nous* may have been inspired by Brecht. But we know that during the Popular Front such avant-garde experiments were little emulated and not at all theorized by French left artists.[27] We may better understand Renoir's film project from his expression of delight with the scenes in *La Marseillaise* between his brother Pierre (Louis XVI) and Lise Delamare (Marie Antoinette): "When I wrote and shot the scenes at the Tuileries, I had the feeling that it might really have happened that way, that it was close to reality."[28]

Using this kind of language, Renoir seems to embrace the narrowness of PCF aesthetic preferences that focused on an aesthetic of realism associated since at least the middle of the nineteenth century with bourgeois artistic practices. According to the old base-superstructure paradigm, the spheres of both party politics and of culture, among other aspects of the superstructure, were determined variously in the immediate or in the last instance by socioeconomic relations (base). Ordinarily, therefore, realist art portrayed the traditional class enemy and, perhaps, workers' resistance. In the face of the fascist threat, however, and in exchange for needed political cooperation with the progressive bourgeoisie, the PCF, trying to "behave," acting the *bon enfant*, heaped praise on the culture of the middle class. Culture, it seemed, though derivative of the deeper socioeconomic processes, was, in the end, of secondary importance, or at least negotiable.[29]

The PCF's embrace of, and deep involvement with, *la civilisation française* from the party's founding (actually from the first founding of the united Socialist party, the Section Française de l'Internationale Ouvrière [SFIO] in 1905) to at least May of 1968 cannot just have been opportunism, a momentary liaison with the painted harlot of bourgeois art. The reasons were more sociological: How could the PCF encourage both cultural innovation—the serious foolery of their temporary friends, the surrealists, for example—and keep their rapport with their constituencies?[30] How could they expect workers and peasants to assimilate to a moving, confusing avant-garde cultural scene? Better to read the Molière and Jean Racine assigned in the republican school, to buy classics in handsome bindings, display them, perhaps read some. Better to learn to appreciate the gothic, Victor Hugo, champagne. Thus, in 1937, on the three hundredth anniversary of the publication of his *Discourse on Method*, the Communist press joined heartily with the bourgeois newspapers in praise of René Descartes's contributions to French civilization. Alexander Trachtenberg wrote in his foreword to the English-language translation of "Thorez's Report to the PCF Nineteenth Congress": "The Nineteenth Congress of the French Communist Party was held December 25 to 29, 1937, in the ancient city of Arles, in Provence, in the south of France. This city, in which relics of Roman and Greek civilization still stand, and which is the cradle of French culture, was a fitting place for such a congress, symbolizing the role of the Communists as the true inheritors and defenders of the best traditions of their country."[31] That year, too, *L'Humanité*, the PCF newspaper, celebrated Rouget de Lisle, the composer of the national anthem, La Marseillaise.

The explanation for the party's embrace of bourgeois culture and its associated aesthetic forms lies, I believe, in the historic social role of the party as an important mediator of social promotion. Itself often treated as an outsider in French life, the PCF sought to be accepted as belonging, and it attracted to its ranks many gifted people with similar status concerns, above all immigrants, but also peasants from red regions, lower white-collar workers in private and state employ, and, of course, thoughtful workers. Remarkably, in 1930s France, there was only the choice between high culture and no culture. So, if workers and peasants could immerse themselves and their children in the culture of France, that is, of Paris—the language, the arts, and the *doxa* (verities) of French life, to use Pierre Bourdieu's word—they would be fully French.[32] Recall that the action of the film *La Marseillaise* moves from the south to Paris: from the provinces to the capital, from the periphery of the revolution to its center. Paris was where France was made and remade.

The organized Left played a complicated game. Wrapping itself in the traditions of the nation was perhaps necessary at that juncture, but the neoconservative Right—Maurice Barrès, Charles Maurras, and the

Action Française, to name the most influential cultural figures—had for more than thirty years claimed that mantel. At the time of the Dreyfus Affair, Maurras formulated the intellectual strategy of the Right that finally so well served the Vichy government in 1940. He denounced the government of the republic as merely the *legal* France. The *real* France lay rather in the cultural discourse of the Right, as it spoke in the name "of the land and of the dead" of the nation, to use Barrès's ghoulish image for French tradition. In the thirties, Maurras hammered away in his newspaper *L'action française* explaining that there existed a gap between the legal country and the real country; electoral results could not possibly represent the will of France. André Thirion and his surrealist friends were infuriated with the frequent echoes of that "shabby and anti-parliamentary nationalism" in "at least half of the metropolitan press."[33]

So paradoxically, the French Communists and Socialists abstained from challenging inherited cultural values even as they brought into question historic class relations. Important cultural spokespeople of the Left, even in statements radically assailing the inheritors of France, continued to think that the paradigm spelled out by Maurras—that there was only one way to be French—held true. Louis Aragon, having totally altered his prose style from surrealism to realism when he broke with his avant-garde friends,[34] described his and the PCF's literary politics this way in his "Defense of the French Novel":

> I deny the quality of *Frenchness* to the prose of Coblenz [the émigré retreat during the revolution], to the prose of the Versaillais [the people who crushed the Paris Commune], to the prose of the seditious elements in 1935 [the radical right suspected of insurrectionary intentions]. Our French novel is French because it expresses the profound spirit of the French People. . . . It is the arm of the true French against the two hundred families who run the banks, the gambling houses, and the brothels.[35]

Aragon was arguing that the PCF and its allies, not the French Right, understood the truth of being French. He did not challenge Maurras's idea that there existed only one truly French culture. His reading the Right out of France made the countermove to the Right's historic tactic of excluding the Left from their vision of France. But as in the rhetorical war about who was supposedly un-American in the 1950s—recall the intense cultivation of down-home American folk music by leftist musicians in response to the Right's campaign to root out the foreign ideology that was communism—the Left lost ground by engaging within such terms of debate.

Contrast this vision of France with André Breton's reply to his former cultural revolutionary companions in the 1935 conference talk he had prepared (which he ended up being barred from giving himself by the conference organizers because he had struck the Soviet author Ilya Ehrenburg on the eve of the conference). Éluard had had to read for him: "We remain opposed to any claim by a Frenchman that he alone possesses the cultural patrimony of France, and to all exaltation of a feeling of Frenchness in France."[36] Breton, and under his influence the surrealist movement, never yielded to nationalism; the surrealists championed a principled internationalism in the interwar decades. As early as 1921—only three years after the war's end—Breton and Aragon had staged a mock trial of Maurice Barrès for unbridled nationalism, with the Unknown Soldier giving testimony against him in German. Breton, Éluard, and Aragon joined the PCF in the late 1920s. The second two stayed and changed their aesthetic styles. Breton, after being asked to report to his party cell on the social and economic conditions of Italian workers, and apparently criticized for not doing a good enough job, left as a consequence of this proletarian hazing.

We may fault the surrealists for lack of political realism, indeed, for being surreal when the moment seemed to call for practical action rather than more aesthetic-ideological manifestos. But in most cases, they made remarkably sound political judgments, including an early, and for France, a prescient, anti-imperialism.[37] Perhaps the political Left committed the greater error: embedding workers and peasants in *la civilisation française*, when the Right had control of that powerful discourse since at least the Dreyfus Affair, could only result in the political and cultural disappointment of the Left and its friends.[38]

YOU CAN'T CHANGE THE RULES OF THE GAME

Soon after he completed *La Marseillaise*, Renoir started *La règle du jeu*, a film that signals the defeat of the Popular Front government, as well

Congratulations all around after the hunt, with killed small animals piled up in a cart. Still from Jean Renoir's *La règle du jeu* (1939). Author's collection.

as that of Renoir's political hopes. The release of this new film in 1939 followed the drift to the right of some of the population and the succeeding governments. Thus *La règle du jeu* is ostensibly about love and not politics. Renoir weaves the story's several love triangles—the marquis, his wife, and her admirer, the aviator; the marquis, his wife, and his mistress; and the gamekeeper, his wife, the maid, and the poacher, to name the principal ones—into a sophisticated comedy of manners that depicts a series of unrequited or impossible loves. All the chasing after unattainable love comes to its denouement in a passionate shooting on the grounds over a betrayal of the heart,[39] an "unfortunate accident," as the marquis labels the killing. In the film's powerful last scene, just after the shooting, as people cluster outside at the spot where it had taken place, the marquis invites the household and his weekend guests back into the château and to their ordered lives.

La règle du jeu deals with an inherited France that was, and will be, a society governed by wealth, class, and status. In the film people shoot

"An unfortunate accident." The marquis invites his guests to reenter the château after his gamekeeper has mistakenly killed the aviator who he thought was his wife's lover. Still from Jean Renoir's *La règle du jeu* (1939). Author's collection.

rabbits and emotional rivals, not class enemies. How far Renoir had retreated may be seen by contrasting those hunting scenes with the simulated newsreel footage in *La vie est à nous* of prosperous-looking bourgeois taking target practice at human-figure targets. In the earlier film, the armed rich gunning down human figures certainly and starkly signaled class war.

The 1939 film asks, what does love have to do with it? And, uncharacteristically, Renoir answers, "nothing!" In the context of Renoir's oeuvre, this, perhaps his most brilliant work, signified his descent into hopelessness about changing French society.[40] He had believed that *les copains*, the old buddies, of the Popular Front could bring love by means of politics. They could not. The rules of the powerful and the rich had held.

La règle du jeu failed both at the box office and with the uncomprehending critics. Moreover, the government banned it soon after its disastrous release as too demoralizing to show in those tense prewar days. So in August of that year, 1939, Renoir gratefully accepted the invitation of the Italian government to come to Rome to do a film to be titled *La Tosca*. But war with Germany loomed on the horizon, and before filming began, Renoir was called back home in September to do his military service in the cinematic service of the army. His superiors immediately sent him back to Italy to continue work on the film. This gesture was part of a larger effort of the desperate French government to persuade Mussolini not to support Hitler in the imminent German attack on France. But when Germany invaded France in June 1940, the Italian army moved in from the southeast. Renoir hastily returned to Paris only to become one of the millions of refugees fleeing the German army rolling almost unopposed on Paris. Now with France defeated and German troops occupying Paris, Renoir remained at his family home just outside Nice. Friends were leaving the country; the French film industry was in disarray.

Renoir thought hard about how and where he wanted to live. Soon after the change of regime, Renoir had written to a Vichy official saying flattering things about Marshal Pétain. But his Leftist past made the new principled far-Right regime uninterested in him. But then Otto Abetz, the new German ambassador and a great admirer of French culture, sent representatives to ask Renoir to work in a new German-sponsored film corporation. Renoir did not want to, but to refuse was out of the question, perhaps even dangerous. So he left Europe and went to Hollywood, there to become an increasingly "Hollywood" director. Politics were not the way to the harmony Renoir sought. Political strife had forced him into exile. Yet we may find his postwar interest in Asian contemplative values already prefigured in the space between *La Marseillaise* and *La règle du jeu*.[41]

THE RIVER

The river of the title is the Ganges, and the film is set in postwar India. Beautifully shot, *The River* was Renoir's first color film, and in many critics' eyes, his best American work. The style was his now finely tuned poetic realism: Along a stretch of the Ganges live British and Indians, some intermarried and all working side by side in a kind of third world echo of the cultural mixing of *Toni.* In the film the river serves not as a way to connect to other areas, but rather as a place and a state of soul.

The River tells of the relationships and loves of three young women coming of age. At one point, a handsome wounded American war veteran, Captain John, arrives to convalesce at the home of his cousin, a retired Anglo-Indian. The young women all get adolescent crushes on the brave captain. Harriet, the oldest, but perhaps the least emotionally mature of them, throws herself in the river to end a pyschological tension she cannot endure. Captain John jumps in and saves her life. In a subplot, Harriet's little brother, Bogey, and a Hindu playmate try to imitate the snake charmers in the village; Bogey is bitten by the cobra and dies. And the wife of the British factory manager, Harriet's and Bogey' mother, pregnant with her seventh child at the film's beginning, gives birth finally to a girl.

So we see the story of a community of different origins living in peace in an Asian Eden. They live from the processing of jute, organic fibers. Their existences blend like the tributaries of the Ganges along whose shores they dwell. In this small world along the river, they are born, they love, they give birth, and they die, as people along that shore did in the past and will forever into the future. Captain John, the only source of social excitement in the film, finally leaves. And the peaceful river flows on.

India had become independent in August 1947. Renoir made the film on location three years later, in 1950. He was filming while communal riots still erupted, yet nothing in the film transcends the everyday lives of people living near a jute factory that provides most of them their jobs and livelihoods. The local fishermen ply their trade as they have always done; we see no pre- or postindependence meetings or demonstrations, no anti-imperialist rhetoric, no intercommunal tensions, no class conflict in the jute factory. "People [were] very tired of war, of privation, of fear and of doubt," he said in his 1952 piece in the *Cahiers du Cinéma.* While making the film—"even as the Hindus and Mohametans were killing each other"—he and his film companions felt the dawning of an age of "good will" [bienveillance]. "The smoke of burning houses did not smother our confidence."[42] More about the everyday even than *Toni,* which gave a clear rendering of the unjust social relations at the quarry, *The River* is desperately about inner peace.

Why did Captain John suddenly show up in India at the crisis moment of independence? Might he have been an American secret agent? No, Captain John had found the United States to which he had first returned after World War II too modern, too materialist. He had come to India seeking the tranquility not found in the West. In the film, he serves only as the plot device of the handsome stranger who sows emotional disorder. Captain John had nothing to do with the Colonel Landsdale character in Graham Greene's almost contemporary novel, *The Quiet American* (1956). But he was there for a political purpose nevertheless.

Captain John was played (very poorly) by Thomas Breen, the son of Joseph Breen, the conservative Catholic head of the Hollywood Production Code. Renoir made the film in the era of the Hollywood Red Scare. Brecht, Renoir's friend, had just been summoned to testify before the House Un-American Activities Committee, and, after his appearance, without even going home to pack, had immediately fled to Europe. Young Breen was there as Renoir's anti-Communist insurance. Maybe the whole scenario came from the same fear and caution— maybe the film was Renoir's way of shutting out the unpromising postwar and postcolonial world.[43]

Bogey died of a snakebite, trying to imitate his Indian playmate. Captain John, the personification of the West, of imperialism, came, made a small flurry in people's lives, and then—like the British raj—left India. He left little trace: he had saved the young girl from drowning, but he had been the cause of her attempted suicide. The river which watered the ancient civilization flowed on and on, unchanged and unchangeable.

CONCLUSION

How did Renoir move from the multicultural and contested world of the northern shore of the Mediterranean to revolutionary and patriotic Paris and finally to the world-isolated peace of the banks of the Ganges? Biographers have suggested that the women in his life turned this suggestive man toward the different political winds of his career. Maybe, but the contrary might hold just as true: he could have chosen his companions to fit who he was at the moment. Renoir was always sensitive to his environment. The worlds in which he lived changed radically during his career; for the supreme purpose of making his films, he went along, as best he could. In the 1930s, for example, it was hard to get financing for a film in the closed French film industry, especially for a relative outsider like Renoir. Renoir may have seen the PCF and its members as both sources of funding and of audiences in difficult times. At the moment the party was bringing together all progressive forces against fascism, they wanted his cultural capital as the greatest living French filmmaker. He needed their money and their numbers. It was an exchange of capitals which, if not made in heaven, at least profited both partners. Vichy did not want him. If he didn't work for the Germans, he could not stay. He was not attracted by the Gaullists in London either.

So he went to the United States, where at least he could continue working. When after the war he made *The River* in faraway India with American financing, he could leave behind the increasingly dangerous —for him—politicized world of his adapted country. The French film industry had not yet recovered from the war years. Renoir had no stomach for returning to his homeland to face in the Fourth Republic something very much like the intense social tensions of his interwar years. He wished to make the Ganges his river too.

When he did return to Paris in 1954, he made *French Cancan*, a handsome color film about the riotous 1880s, when ex-laundresses won admirers by dancing the cancan at the new Moulin Rouge. *The River* had been an escape to the peaceful East. *French Cancan* was Renoir's escape back to his own youth in Montmartre of the Belle Epoque. The world had been so joyous and simple then: just passion, music, and dance. The splendid production number of the dance that gave his film its name—to Renoir's relief and joy—pleased all the Paris critics.[44]

Renoir himself should have the last word. The filmmaker had been at a moment actively engaged on the Left in politics, but he had never been among the avant-garde of aesthetic experiments. At perhaps the most hopeful political moment of the twenty years between the two wars, he had this to say about style and invention in film: "It's not about being avant-garde; rather it's a question of making no films [*rien tourner*] that do not come directly from the heart."[45] But I am not arguing that any kind of aesthetic style is more or less prophylactic against fascism, or attractive to the Left. Newness in politics is by no means connected to newness in art. As Tom Gunning put it, "By the fifties, he [Renoir] turned against the aspects of modernity which had earlier so excited him. He now denounced the pace of modern life and technological change, and longed for pastoral idylls. . . . The utopian energy of the Twenties contrasts with the desire in the Fifties to retreat into natural and primitive refuges from a global technology which no longer carries any promise of adventure or fulfillment."[46] This discussion of the period surrounding Renoir's great political films has permitted us to identify the three social elements of Renoir's social cinema. We have seen the role of the habitus of the filmmaker, here Renoir's vision of France as a community of *copains*. Second, in discussing the contested field of the meaning of Revolution, we have drawn the horizon of social and aesthetic meaning that French viewers brought with them to the movie theater and that seem the kinds of capital at play in the field of filmmaking. We have also had a chance to see how the institution of art of the 1930s both empowered one aesthetic and made others impossible. In each case, focusing on the interaction of the creative with the social field illuminated both sides of the border.

Finally, the work of Renoir has given us a special optic on the conflict over what was France and who spoke for the nation in the last days of the French Republic. In *La vie est à nous* and *La Marseillaise* he envisioned a utopian France of friends and neighbors, a community of the people of the republic. This was the Popular Front's authentic France. But Marshal Pétain and some of his followers imagined a national community of *la terre et les morts*, of the land and its dead, as the real nation. Renoir's search for the real France, and his realization that the Right controlled its rules, finally caused him to become disillusioned with politics. With the intense contests for political domination between the Gaullists and Communists in the immediate postwar years, the moment of *fraternité* had passed. The French film industry was in disarray; it would be hard to work. He stayed in Hollywood. Hollywood was not France, but it was not the site of his greatest regrets either. When Hollywood became unsafe, and the United States became too mechanical, too modern, he fled, like some other contemporary Westerners, to a peaceful colonial world along the Ganges where the eternal human cycle seemed still to hold sway, for just a little time longer. In a grand and elegant manner, Renoir expressed the post–World War II longing in the West for a world without tumultuous cities, without social conflict, without politics. The temptations of the romantic Orient had always existed to distract the people in the West from fighting for a better world at home.

4

FRANCE'S BLACK VENUS

For all of aesthetic modernism's self-contained Europeness, and for all of colonialism's farawayness, the two activities were twinned. In parallel fashion they rose in the mid-nineteenth century, flourished for about a hundred years, and crashed together in the third quarter of the twentieth. But it is not at all clear what the elective affinities between these disparate phenomena might mean, if anything. After all, for a time in the nineteenth century, the business cycle really did vary with outbursts of sunspot activity on the sun—until it didn't anymore. The common periodicity, which could have been judged a result of better harvests due to more sun, so more food to eat, more grain to sell, more raw materials for manufacture, and so on, turned out to be just a temporary association.

In this essay, I will demonstrate that in France, at least, there really existed a covariation between the rise, triumph, and decline of aesthetic modernism and the life-cycle of French colonialism. That is interesting and, I believe, not hard to show. But I wish to argue, further, that the two reciprocally potentialized each other.[1] In other words, no French colonialism, no aesthetic modernism; no aesthetic modernism, no empire building. It is not that they caused each other; that is not my claim. But rather, a common factor, a degraded European modernity—Jürgen Habermas's incomplete project of modernity—made them both, linked them, and drove the dialectically reinforcing effect.

First, so that we might all be on the same page when I speak of modernism in the arts, let me begin with some qualities marked by

Habermas: "The spirit and discipline of aesthetic modernism assumed clear contours in the work of Baudelaire. Modernity then unfolded in various avant-garde movements and finally reached its climax in the Café Voltaire of the dadaists and in surrealism. Aesthetic modernity is characterized by attitudes which find a common focus in a changing consciousness of time."[2] In the second half of the nineteenth century, aesthetic modernism was invented in France. We see it first in poetry and painting. It was the reaction to, or better, the symptom of, a parallel new social modernism. The period of the rise and triumph of French modernism, the early years of the Third Republic, at the same time marked the defining moment of French colonialism. The new modernity in art of course depended on the isolation of form from content, on the parallel isolation of art from society, and on the invention of new language and new ways of seeing to make a new way of being.[3] But most important, as Habermas remarked, modernism complicated the dimension of time in art. E. P. Thompson's splendid article on the new discipline of clock-time during the Industrial Revolution tells of the birth of this new tyranny of mechanical time: with big clocks everywhere, and the new pocket watches absolutely essential for a smoothly functioning factory society.[4] Cultural reactionaries, like Thomas Carlyle, refused the new measure of duration. But not just them. Moderns also rebelled against the mechanical, supposedly objective, evenly spaced intervals of industrialism's timepieces. They wanted a time that was subjective, malleable, even a time that could be forgotten, to reveal a form out of time. This essay follows a similar pattern: it will not attempt a narrative of continuous, unbroken development. Rather, key—if discontinuous—moments and significant—if not immediately related—actors in the history of modernism have guided my account. Let me try to make this point more concretely.

Here I propose to ask the poet of modern life, Charles Baudelaire, to help us understand the connection of modernity and colonialism.[5] In this instance, I cannot agree with Walter Benjamin's characterization of the poet's work. Benjamin says of Baudelaire that "he envisioned blank spaces which he filled in with his poems. His work cannot merely be categorized as historical, like anyone else's, but it intended to be so and understood itself as such."[6] Benjamin's Baudelaire essay deals with the crowd of the modern city, an important theme in the poetry. The city poetry speaks of leaving that crowd, starting again, making a new world on a blank sheet of paper.

I think, rather, that Baudelaire searched for ways to escape history. For him modernity was discontinuous; the past meant nothing. His poetry communicates an intense and rich immersion in the moment, the now. He took a momentary interest in socialist politics during the revolution of 1848; he went into the streets with some of his literary friends. But we learn something of his motives when a friend reported seeing him excitedly waving a rifle looted from a gun shop. On catching sight of the man, Baudelaire shouted to him that they must find General Aupick (his stepfather) and shoot him. They couldn't; he didn't. And Oedipal dramas, I think, however psychologically revealing, do not count as political engagement.

Robert D. E. Burton has tried to follow the zigzag of Baudelaire's political convictions. His is a carefully nuanced study, but I am not persuaded that we can construct a political history of the poet's mind based on snatches of poetry and, occasionally, sentences in his letters. Burton uses phrases like "the general trajectory of Baudelaire's political thinking," and "it seems to me," and "plausible"—all just on the first page of his conclusion—to close his case. The mundane reality was that Baudelaire never voted, never joined a political group, and never took a strong or consistent parti pris for a specific political outcome. His was rather a politics of the moment, or, if you will, of mood swings.[7]

But Baudelaire did deeply feel the ravages of historical change; he wanted both to vicariously dip into that boiling sea and to find ways to escape to dry land. That island of safety was ahistorical modernism. He seemed to revel in the violence of his times, but the programmatic social radicalism of the Paris workers offended him. The rudeness of the revolutionaries of 1848 evoked in him an abiding distaste for all democratic politics. And after, and because of, the June Days of street fighting and barricades, Baron Georges-Eugène Haussmann demolished much of historic Paris to replace it with another city, Benjamin's "capital of the nineteenth century."[8] Baudelaire's *flâneur*, a man all dressed up with nowhere special to go, strolled this massive scene of demolition and new construction. The workers' violent attempt to create a new *cité*, followed by Napoleon III's destruction and reshaping of Paris, both shocked Baudelaire.

Baron Haussmann's destruction of old Paris. Leveling the site for the wide Prince Eugène boulevard. With the permission of the Bibliothèque Nationale de France.

Baudelaire's poetry also turned away from the dense and eventful history of the Paris of the middle decades of the nineteenth century. The blank spaces that excited Baudelaire, where the poet could create a world, did not exist in Paris. With sweat, stone, and iron and following a cold instrumental rationality, Baron Haussmann was both making and filling real blank places in the city. Nor did the free spaces Baudelaire wanted exist in the palimpsest that was the historic France in an old Europe. The mysterious and timeless colonial world became, to adapt T. S. Eliot's phrase, an "objective correlative" of Baudelaire's art.[9] The virgin map of Africa was just being written on as he wrote his poems. Explorers like René Caillé, Linant de Bellefonds, and Paul de Chaillu were giving names to rivers and lakes, peoples and animals, and to vast regions. In more charted regions like Senegal, governors like General Louis Faidherbe were labeling new ethnic and geographic facts they had just created.

The practice of making conquered peoples employ new languages and new designations for their homelands is not infrequent in European history. Brian Friel's wonderful play *Translations* (1980) is about the British sending soldiers to their Irish possession completely to remap and to rename its surface. The great Ordinance Survey of Ireland (1833) took place just a few years before Baudelaire started writing. In a passage in Friel's play, Hugh, a hedge schoolmaster, is speaking to an English lieutenant, there to take linguistic possession of the land: "And it can happen—to use an image you'll understand—it can happen that a civilization can be imprisoned in a linguistic contour which no longer matches the landscapes of . . . fact."[10] In Baudelaire's day, France and the other imperialist lands of Europe were also writing on Africa and Indochina as if on blank sheets of paper. The linguistic contours they set down in Africa and Asia made the indigenous peoples of the empire strangers in their own homes. Peoples without history, as the nineteenth century put it—or, more accurately, people robbed of their history—they lived in places where Europeans could start again, without the burden of their own past or that of the conquered. The colonial empire, like the new creative modernism, offered European artists a clean slate. Note the workings of a kind of a colonial unconscious in Habermas's choice of metaphors for characterizing aesthetic modernism, "The avant-garde understands itself as invading unknown territory, exposing itself to the dangers of sudden, shocking encounters, conquering an as yet unoccupied future. The avant-garde must find a direction in the landscape into which no one seems to have yet ventured."[11]

From his earliest years Baudelaire himself was deeply drawn to colonial things. T. Denean Sharpley-Whiting traces the figure of the African prostitute of his prose poem "La belle Dorothée" to a woman's picture in the travel book entitled *Voyage dans l'intérieur de l'Afrique*, written by his great uncle François Le Vaillant. The thirteen-year-old Charles had asked his mother to give him a copy.[12] Also, when he was still a child, his stepfather, a major in the army, fought for nearly two years pacifying Algerian resistance to French rule. Major Aupick was promoted to lieutenant colonel for his part in the French victories. Then immediately in 1831, just after France had formally annexed Algeria, he was reassigned to crush the rebellion of the silk weavers in Lyon. Both the Algerian rebels and the Lyon silk workers fought against the new French modern then coming to life. The North Africans resisted a colonial future. The Canuts defied an industrial capitalist destiny. Baudelaire disliked his mother's new husband, but his rejection of his soldier stepfather did not take the psychologically possible form of support for the peoples the man had conquered.

Of course, there were others in historically privileged social stations who regretted the changes to France, especially the passing of old cherished amenities. Through the middle third of the century, some young men born of high bourgeois families invented the transgressive persona of the dandy. How transgressive? Well—bourgeois horror— they neither worked nor saved! Their incomes came from old money or investments in land. Or their fathers were well placed in state service, as was the case of Baudelaire's family. They dressed elegantly in clothing that made it almost impossible to perform any activity other than strolling or sitting and talking in cafés. They transgressed without risk.[13] Baudelaire's own definition of the dandy, self-serving though it may be, was insightful: "Dandyism arises especially in periods of transition, when democracy is not yet all powerful and aristocracy is only partially tottering or brought low. In the disturbance of such periods a certain number of men, detached from their own class, disappointed and disoriented, but still rich in native energy, may form a project of founding a new sort of aristocracy."[14] We see here a premature Nietzscheanism. Or more accurately, Friedrich Nietzsche's new *Übermensch* would be, in part, what the philosopher had learned from Baudelaire.

To take him away from what they condemned as his debauched life and his bad friends, Baudelaire's parents put him on a slow boat bound for Calcutta. Baudelaire had always been fascinated by the East. But apparently not by long and boring boat trips—he jumped ship when they reached the island of Mauritius, off the southeastern coast of Africa. There he stayed for a time with a French-speaking Creole couple. He wrote love poems to the wife—with the permission of her husband—praising the woman's exotic beauty so magnificently set off in the tropical surroundings. One poem ended with a wish that she might someday join him in Paris. And if she were ever to come, "You would summon forth a thousand sonnets in the hearts of the poets, / Who your glances would make more submissive than your blacks."[15] He had left Bordeaux for the Indies at the end of May 1841 at the age of twenty. He returned only in February 1843. Although he never got to the subcontinent, for the rest of his life it was important for him to

Caricature of Charles
Baudelaire by Nadar.
With the permission
of the Bibliothèque
Nationale de France.

claim that he had experienced India in all its strangeness. Enid Starkie, his biographer, writes of Baudelaire that "he came back from the East with a romantic yearning for rich, warm countries, for exotic splendor, and beauty impossible to achieve in this world. . . . This journey to the East was the turning-point of Baudelaire's life."[16]

When he reestablished himself in Paris as the young dandy living now on a windfall inheritance, he immediately took a striking mistress. She was an African French sometime actress, Jeanne Duval, a *Mulatto* in the French of his day; she became the Black Venus in the cycle of poems with that name in *Les fleurs du mal*. We know very little true about her; she went by different names. She does not have a voice of her own in any of the eyewitness accounts of Baudelaire's life. It is not certain what she looked like.[17] It was as if he had created her first for the sake of his dandyism, then for his poetry, and finally for his psyche.[18] He portrayed her as his rude and sensual muse. He accused her of being cruel and unfaithful to him to anyone who would listen or read his letters. Yet at a moment of straiten means, Baudelaire sent her into the streets to earn them some money. A little knowledge of the mono-maniacal way he conducted his frenzied Parisian life—including once knocking her down, which cut open her head, and then, instead of helping her, running away—suggests that, on the contrary, it was Baudelaire who cruelly oppressed *her*. Nevertheless, she remained for him the closest to a long-term, if punctuated, love that he ever knew.

That life, that relationship, has much in it of the larger relation between the French bourgeoisie and the colonial empire. In "The Negress in the Brothel," the surrealist René Clevel evoked this connection: "the lecher in his lust to possess . . . cannot rise above the simple notion of an act of annexation." Along the same line, he pointed to Baudelaire's absolute need for Jeanne Duval, the black whore, to make him feel superior and in charge.[19] Classicism promulgated universal norms. Romantics were more interested in the unique. But the Other—Baudelaire's wild mulatta woman—could be born only of the union of aesthetic modernism and colonial encounters.[20]

By the first years of the Third Republic, we may see the modernist bifurcation of praxis and righteousness crystallize, to varying degrees of hardness, in bourgeois economic analysis, in the crass interest politics of the day, and in the institutions of discipline and punishment treated by Michel Foucault. And, of course, in art for art's sake. For all their talk of the civilizing mission, the French champions of the colonial enterprise had also to separate the conquest and the subjugation—that is, making indigenous peoples of Africa and Asia into French-defined subjects—from any moral principles that might have commanded them to stop in guilt. It was just the disjuncture between the facts of empire and the colonialists' self-serving uplifting discourse that the colonized could readily see and one day would turn against their conquerors. In the nineteenth century, France could no longer win glory and art booty in European wars; the mission to civilize the benighted peoples of Africa and Asia promised national renewal and glory for the republic.

Many Third Republic writers, especially of the *récit de voyage* (travel writing) genre, narcissistically explored their literary selves in the lands of the colonial Other. In *The Modernist Traveler* Kimberley Healey demonstrates how in the first three decades of the twentieth century authors such as Victor Segalen, Paul Morand, Blaise Cendrar, Paul Nizan, Paul-Jean Toulet, Albert Londres, Ernest Psichari, Henri Mi-

Fantasy by unknown artist of Charles Baudelaire with Jeanne Duval.
With the permission of the Bibliothèque Nationale de France.

chaux, Alexandra David-Neel, and Isabelle Eberhardt caught the
modernist infection in the course of their exposure to colonial places.
And traces of that modernism—the anomie and the freedom of an
uncertain self, disorientation and yet wonder at the speed of movement
and of change, creation of imagined zones—but separate from it—from
materials of the real, and a new metaphysic of the body—thereafter
remained, like malaria, with them. We find the effects of their exposure
to the colonial in their writings.[21]

Painters and sculptors, as well, "discovered" North and West Africa
and the Pacific Islands again and again in the late nineteenth and early
twentieth centuries.[22] We see that with the fauvists, and soon thereafter, with cubism. Already early in the new century Paul Cézanne had

Pablo Picasso in his atelier at the Bateau Lavoir in Paris with African statues behind him. Photo by Burgess Gelett, 1908. Collection of the ACHAC, Paris.

commented, "Geometric abstraction, that's Negro art." And because we are speaking of *the* movement in which the invention of the new is primary, there was, and is, dispute about who, among the fauvists first integrated this "Negro art," meaning then all "primitive," non-European art, into his work.

Did Pablo Picasso get his ideas from postcards with photographs of African women found in his archives? Or did he discover Africa when he visited the Paris ethnographic museum? He attended the 1900 Paris Exposition; African art and artifacts were displayed there. Or was Henri Matisse's presenting Gertrude Stein a Vili sculpture from Bakongo more important for the genealogy of French primitivism? Matisse had seen it in the window of a little antique shop one day on his way to her Rue de Fleurus apartment, and had impulsively bought it for a few francs. Picasso, who was at the Stein salon that day, was much taken by the piece. Max Jacob reported walking into Picasso's studio the next morning and finding the floor covered with cubist-style drawings of the head. Jacob dates the beginnings of cubism to this moment. Other drawings of heads came later, and then sometime soon after the

A Still from Jean-Jacques Annaud's film *Black and White in Color* (1976). "The Republic Needs You," announced the sergeant—recruiting during World War I in the Ivory Coast. Author's collection.

painter began his famous *Demoiselles d'Avignon* (1907–9) with the faces of the prostitutes of the Spanish brothel portrayed in the likeness of African masks.

But the faces of the women of the Barcelona house resembled four different African styles, not just that of the Vili. Picasso liked the form and geometric qualities of African carvings, while his great contemporary Matisse was taken by the strong colors and patterns used in North Africa and the Pacific Isles. It is not very important to this essay to decide who was first, or even how; that kind of problematic is more a residual artifact of the modernist practice of crowning the first artist to introduce a formal innovation than it is a burning historical issue. But from the new modernism in the art of the turn of the century until the end of colonialism, "primitivism" never disappeared from the high modernist canon. Works by artists from onetime colonial societies is another story, one best told as part of the history of the postmodern and the postcolonial. Let us pass on to the Negrophilia of the interwar years.[23]

Jean Cocteau, parasol bearer to boxer Al Brown and others in 1930, on the
eve of Brown's boxing match to raise money for the Paris Ethnography
Museum's collecting expedition to Africa, the Mission Dakar-Djibouti
headed by Marcel Griaule. Before departing, Griaule emceed the match.
Collection of the ACHAC, Paris.

The colonial troops that France threw into World War I aided
France's holding out in that barbaric struggle. Most of the time they
performed menial rear-line duties—clearing mine fields, carrying sup-
plies and digging trenches and graves—but for big offensives, they were
often sent out of the trenches first, ahead of the white soldiers, to
absorb the initial withering fire. The Germans mobilized no such colonial levies to send against the British and French machine guns. The
European nations, Britain and France, who had brought troops from
their populous colonies to fight the European's war, won.

At the war's end, the colonial troops who had come to France to
defend and to die for their second homeland, and also to discover it,

In feathers, Josephine
Baker presents her new
1925 review in Paris.
Collection of the
ACHAC, Paris.

were summarily sent back without the grant of French citizenship they
had been promised. Both they and those who died left behind their
ghosts. *Négrophilie*—African arts, hot jazz, sensual dances, new songs,
food labels, posters, and enchantment with the irrational and the passion attributed to "Negro culture"—swept through all the levels of
Parisian society.

Saint Louis–born Josephine Baker, for example, dazzled audiences
with her wild, supposedly African dances and her displays of raw sexuality in shows like *Le tumulte noir* and *La revue nègre*, as well as in her
films. Her appearances acted out French whites' fantasies about black
Africa, and so contributed nothing of value to the actual understanding
of the continent or of its diaspora. Everyone who writes on her makes
this criticism. Certainly, from having lived so much historical travail in
the aftermath of European decolonization and the U.S. civil rights
movement—in which, by the way, Baker played an active role—we see
such criticisms as valid.

But she had as fans the gratin of twentieth-century international modernism: among others, Picasso, Jean Cocteau, Le Corbusier, George-Henri Rivière, Michel Leiris, Jean-Paul Sartre, Simone de Beauvoir, Alexander Calder, e. e. cummings, Gertrude Stein, and Kurt Weill. It is unlikely that such sophisticated people believed that the lives of Africans or American blacks had much to do with what they saw on stage. No, they found a new Europe at her stage shows, not a mysterious Africa. Baker evoked a set of powerful values, a mise-en-scène of a fictitious black culture that these white intellectuals knew they badly needed: connecting the mind and body; learning to appreciate difference; connecting to their own deep inner feelings of creativity, sensuality, and desire; not to omit the longing for freedom; and the courage to resist the despair of ever gaining it. Baker teased her appreciative modernists fans with glimpses of France's unconscious. Elizabeth Ezra has aptly termed it France's "colonial unconscious," remarking on all the ambivalences found therein. It was this unconscious that twentieth-century modernism prized as the prime workshop of creativity. Yes, as Ezra emphasizes, Baker performed the primitive for her French public; she acted the "floating signifier of cultural difference."[24] But by helping white French audiences release a buried part of their common, if often very flawed, humanity, Baker helped them realize a larger, more inclusive, vision of that unity. In this most unlikely way, too, Africa and the descendents of its kidnapped peoples offered the French vital instruction about the unrealized potential of French culture.

Even in her sound films, Baker performed the ambivalences of French colonialism. In *Princesse Tam Tam* (dir. Edmond de Gréville, 1935) she plays the black exotic sex object. In the scenario, de Mirecourt, a blocked white writer who goes to Africa hoping there to free his creativity, meets a street woman. He makes her his muse. Baker plays the demeaning and racialized child-whore in the film. In Africa de Mirecourt does indeed manage to finish his novel, wonderfully titled *Civilisation*, and it becomes a best seller in France. His new literary success permits him to leave the colonies for Paris to reestablish his marriage and to continue his now productive literary life. Aouina, Princess Tam Tam's given name, follows him to Paris but cannot stay. The magical pull of her homeland is too strong, and she goes home. There she marries a swarthy North African type (a white actor in bad brown makeup). She soon bears him a mixed-blood baby. In the film's

Josephine Baker in front
of an art deco jungle
image. Around 1925.
Collection of the ACHAC,
Paris.

last scene, amid a disarray of discarded books and grazing farm animals,
we see a cow contentedly chewing the title page of de Mirecourt's
novel.[25]

Yes, Baker's character had happily reverted to the savage; no Pyg-
malion story here. Assimilation is impossible. As in her other films,
and to Baker's expressed chagrin, the black colonial Venus and the
white European can never have a permanent love. And yet, the film's
tidy conclusion undermines itself. For the source of de Mirecourt's
revived creativity is Africa: without the colonies, without Aouina, no
novel. France needs the colonial—at least in this film—to end its cultural depression. Moreover, the film protests too much on the impossibility of union with the colonial Other. The flimsy narrative evokes a
new cultural possibility, and then forbids it.[26] But how well, how long,
could this film's puny *Interdit!* hold?

Negrophilia spread like an epidemic in the interwar years, but unlike
earlier fades, for example, eighteenth-century *chinoiserie* or the late

nineteenth-century Japanese craze, it never disappeared from French cultural life. Thankfully, with more frequent and more human interactions in subsequent decades, its expression gradually became more empathetic to issues that Africans and African Americans thought important.[27] But also in the interwar years we begin to see in metropolitan France the stirrings of anticolonialism among students from the colonies and in French artists' and intellectuals' circles. Prompting such new forbidden thoughts was the insurgency in Morocco, where Marshal Henri Pétain, the hero of World War I, needed to field 150,000 troops to defeat the rebellious Riffs under Abd-el-Krim. Then, too, two major colonial uprisings in Indochina (Vietnam, in fact) in 1930 were bloodily put down by French troops armed with the most modern weapons and employing airplanes to bomb and strafe rebellious villages. The French military practiced the new techno-terrorist modern warfare a full half decade before Germans and Italian flyers perfected their own new mechanical-killing skills on Spanish Republican villages.

The colonial borrowings and the anticolonialism of the surrealists, I think, occupied the center of that arts movement. They showed a deep understanding of the dominant culture they were challenging, and its relation to empire. The surrealists appreciated how "romantic exoticism and modern travel lust" helped naturalize colonial rule.[28] So much has been written about the surrealist discovery of the exotic Other, it does not need much elaboration here. Around the turn of the century, along with Picasso, they began visiting the Paris ethnography museum to see the suddenly visible African art there. Then they went to watch Josephine Baker dance, seeing in her confirmation of their search for creativity in the noncivilized, the physical, and the unconscious.[29] Like this artist of the life forces, the colonial provided the avant-garde both a formal influence and a model for how to mine the nonrational in life for the sake of new art. Later, in New World exile from Vichy France, the surrealists "discovered" the hitherto mostly ignored (i.e., by the American arts establishment) art of the Amerindians. And our great modernist, Jackson Pollock, carried on their interest in revealing the irrational, the primitive, and the unconscious in his art of swirls, splatters, and drips.[30]

But in the interwar years a powerful strain of fascist modernism also thrived. Perhaps the most creative modernist novelist of the prewar and war years, Louis-Ferdinand Céline, was even before Vichy a hard-line racist fascist in politics. In 1932, he was working as a doctor at a public clinic in Clichy, the part of Paris where the run-down neighborhoods of the poor bordered the sleazy tourist sex district. That year, a year after the great Colonial Exposition, he published his greatest and most avant-garde work, *Voyage au bout de la nuit* (Voyage to the end of the night). He fashioned a writing style to jazzify (*jazzifier*) French literature, as the new sounds of the 1920s had done with French music.

The book's hero, modeled on aspects of the author's life, is wounded in the Great War. He flees Europe to work at an African trading post and then escapes from the wretchedness of Africa to immerse himself in the horrors of industrial life in New York and Detroit. He returns to France to serve as a doctor in the lower depths of the capital. His journeys both geographical and internal simultaneously described the literary itinerary of contemporary social modernity. The destruction of old Europe in the war, the babel of the international city of New York, the human destruction of unbridled industrialism, and, of course, the colonial empire—this was for Céline in 1932 the Via Dolorosa of the modern. His protagonist's taking up colonial trade borrows from the fabled life of Arthur Rimbaud. His passage deep into the bush to find an aberrant employee of the trading company owes something to Joseph Conrad's *Heart of Darkness*. The modernist who hated modernity to the core of his being let his anger give way to moral nihilism and finally to an abiding faith in the racist order of the Nazis.

T. S. Eliot in Britain, the forebears of the New Critics in the American South, Ezra Pound, Filippo Tammaso Marinetti and the Italian futurists, and Ernst Jünger and Stefan George in Germany were all modernists—and far, far to the right. I focus here on the rapport of modernism and colonialism in France, but the relationship, as I have hinted, is worth looking into for other expansionist societies of the period.[31]

Between 1940 and 1944, the feeble government in Vichy made hanging onto the colonies—against allied, German, and especially Japanese threats—a major goal. To undo the work of the Jacobins and their successors in metropolitan France, Vichy encouraged regional languages, modes of dress, dances, songs, and customs. Vichy officials encouraged a parallel right-wing folklorization in the colonies as well.[32]

The methods used to study the societies of Africa, justified by the same salvage metaphor, were beginning to be applied both to provincial France and the far-off possessions. This offers a good example of how hatred of modernity among the traditionalists of Vichy society encouraged them to try to roll back modernism in both metropole and colonies.

At the same time, stylistically conventional novelists like André Malraux in France or the brothers Thomas and Heinrich Mann in Germany resisted fascism, but in work rooted very much in the nineteenth-century realist tradition. I have never been persuaded that any artistic style leads to any specific politics, nor of the contrary. Changes in government allow, even encourage, new arrangements in the aesthetic field. That certainly held true for the changes of power in the aesthetic field of Vichy France and fascist Italy. But the triumphs both of fascist modernism and the new peasant art of the regions of France had no aesthetically formal causes.[33]

French society returned to republican forms after the liberation. Some people in the arts tried to live on the cultural capital accumulated in the century before 1940. This is the setting for Serge Guilbaut's indictment, *How New York Stole the Idea of Modern Art* (from Paris). But this Fourth Republic too much resembled the one that had failed in the interwar years. A return to classicism, with its eternal values, cum modernism, with its tradition of the new, made little sense in the new postwar France. Both classicism and modernism were aesthetically exhausted. I would even hazard the hypothesis, although I cannot pause here to argue it, that the death of modernism in the arts after World War II had something to do with the unhappy fact that most of the great innovating modernists in literature and the other arts had either sided with the enemies of democracy or, like Picasso, admired the Soviet Union. And in any case, neither nineteenth-century classicism nor 1930s modernism fit postwar French society.[34] Might we think of the texts of existentialism—the last stand of the Subject and of a universal world humanist ideal led by a powerful France—as the obituary for the quarreling twins?[35]

With the wave of decolonizations, both violent and plebiscitary, that brought down the Fourth Republic in the late 1950s and early 1960s imperial France completed its dissolution. Modernism expired at the same historical moment. The conjuncture of hopes and events in May

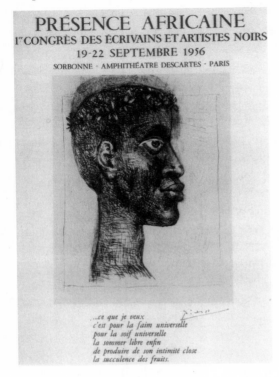

...ce que je veux
c'est pour la faim universelle
pour la soif universelle
la sommer libre enfin
de produire de son intimité close
la succulence des fruits.

Pablo Picasso's drawing for the cover of *Présence Africaine*'s issue on the 1956 conference of black writers and artists. Collection of the ACHAC, Paris.

1968 serves as a good marker of the vast cultural transformations too easily simplified by tacking on a *post-* to the old categories.

In his 1979 *La condition postmoderne: Rapport sur le savoir* (The postmodern condition: Report on knowledge), Jean-François Lyotard confirmed for his Canadian, French, and American readers the death of belief in the great metanarratives of the past. Of course, he meant the progressive ones like Marxism, not the conservative ones like Gaullism or politicized religions. Like Foucault, he formulated the question of changing society in epistemological terms.[36] Lyotard got it right for perhaps some of the arrondissements on the Left Bank, parts of New York and Brooklyn, and spots in Northern California. I am not certain about the rest of Europe and, unfortunately, I do not know the province of Quebec or Latin America well enough to comment on cultural trends in these French culture–friendly regions. What Lyotard would possibly have had to consider zombie metanarratives still seem to inform most public discourse in our nation's capital. But as statisticians say, his N, the number of items in his sample, was shamefully small.

At the beginning of the twentieth century Max Weber defined his contemporary social modernity as the disappearance of magic from the world (*Entzauberung*). But this did not happen all over the world, nor in the way Weber tells it.[37] Certainly from the decade of the 1970s to the present we have seen a global proliferation of magical stories. We continue to hear the innumerable metanarratives, tales about special origins or unique suffering, of identity politics. We continue to hear the many chiliastic religious accounts of the way the world should be ordered: in Islam, especially Shiite forms, exclusionary Hindu nationalism in India, fundamentalist Protestantism, and the late Pope John Paul II's returning to the old pre–Vatican II narratives of faith (especially a recycled Maryology) during his frequent personal missions to Africa and Latin America. In Israel and the United States Jewish young men who wear knitted *kipas* (yarmulkes) and who are willing to take lives of Palestinians in vain, but not the name of "G-d," have armed themselves to fight over pieces of land they are absolutely certain the Deity promised His People. They fight an enemy who they believe will continue to try to destroy Israel unless, like the Tribe of Amulic, they are rooted out, or until the coming of the Messiah.

A glance at a map tracing more than the Métro and RER lines of Paris would show, in respect to places and populations, that the new enthusiasms have most intensely, if not exclusively, gripped both metropole and the third world—the former colonies and spheres of influence of the European powers. I think that Lyotard in his last years had fallen into the despair of the end of ideologies because, once the Marxism of his magazine *Socialisme ou Barbarie* lost meaning for him, he could not think the colonial as a progressive hope in French life, the increasingly loud thing-not-said, the *non-dit*. His metropolitan way of knowing could not help him understand the impact, and transformational possibilities, of the onetime peripheries on the old centers. This symptomatic diagnosis of the aporia in Lyotard's thinking allows us to see the fundamental import of the postmodern impasse: the inability to envision a new world in France.

The moment is right to correct this fundamental *méconnaissance*.

(misrecognition). If we step back a little—as we must sometimes do to really see what is going on in a painting—we will appreciate that *postmodernity* is another word for the postcolonial situation of the metropolitan centers. If society acknowledged the imbrication of the colonial within the metropole, the postmodern within the postcolonial, might not old France make peace with the new France made in the colonies? Might not the millions of the once colonial living in France today be integrated in a new, gloriously united *métissage* [mixity]?[38] The alternative, I fear, is becoming theme-park France with a new currency, the Euro, the bills of which already depict simulacra of typically classical European landscapes and views. But, as if the designers had taken their cues from Jean Baudrillard, these pictures are copies without originals.

Whence this historical amnesia? To misremember four years of Vichy rule and crimes was perhaps understandable for a nation wanting to start again. But to forget a whole colonial empire immediately on its dissolution seems to me, at the very least, careless. How could this happen? While we Americans never tire of discussing the crimes committed in our name, as if guilt talk was equal to actually correcting a past injustice, historical memory in France has tended to erase the unpleasant and the divisive from the national story—until the moment arrives when French intellectuals discuss nothing but a past malfeasance. Alfred Dreyfus's innocence was finally acknowledged—"there is no Dreyfus case," premier Jules Méline had insisted at the height of the affair—and endlessly rehearsed thereafter. After a long silence that ended only with the screening of the *Sorrow and the Pity* (dir. Marcel Ophuls, 1969) in a Left Bank movie theater—which then suffered a mysterious fire—and soon after the publication of American scholar Robert O. Paxton's *Vichy France*, the crimes of Vichy are today at the center of the work of many contemporary historians and institutes in France.[39]

It seems to take at least a generation for a past injustice to resurface for serious discussion in France. This pattern, I believe, has a little to do with limited access to good documentation, and a lot to do with the dying off of the guilty principals. Condemnations of crimes without criminals—at least healthy or living ones—assure a certain degree of justice without causing too much social disruption. Then the evil becomes a problem for historians' endless debates in learned journals, rather than a contemporary one of shameful revelations at sensational trials.[40]

The violent breakup of former Yugoslavia, a historic part of Europe, awoke French intellectuals from their dogmatic slumber. Petty nationalisms, ethnic cleansing, and horrible atrocities—this did not happen only in far away Africa or Indonesia. How removed from Europe were the anguishes of state building and state destroying of so-called third world societies? Maybe some mutual learning was needed? Today, if we go by the growing number of studies done by young French scholars, rising media interest in the former colonial empire, and the polemics in the press in the spring of 2005 over a clause tacked onto a law meant to indemnify refugee Algerian veterans who had fought for France in the Algeria war (*Harkis*), affirming that French imperial rule had benefitted the governed, the time of colonial reckoning has finally come. Over a thousand academic opponents of this arrogant and unjustified historical judgment smuggled into a quite ordinary—even laudable—parliamentary money bill circulated, signed, and had published a petition calling for its repeal.[41]

I think the *méconnaissance* of the colonial heritage also has to do with particular features of the country's relationship to overseas France. Only some twenty-five years after the cutting of formal ties to the colonial empire did we get the first serious study of the old relationship. And that study was done to legitimize forgetting so that France could move on to a new beginning. In 1984, Jacques Marseille published a dense summa on the economic consequences for France of the now devolved colonial dependencies with the unusual title *Empire colonial et capitalisme français: Histoire d'un divorce* (Colonial empire and French capitalism: The history of a divorce).[42] In the spirit of neoliberal analysis, Marseille argued that the decolonization of the late 1950s and early 1960s, rather than injuring the French economy, freed it, as well as the state's budget, from the heavy burdens of both running and subduing the resistance of the colonized. True, a number of old-fashioned consumer industries, long-habituated to the protected colonial market—for example, manufacturers of pots and pans, cheap cotton textiles, low-end leather goods, food staples, and the like—could not survive in the postcolonial era.[43]

Marseille's argument is flawed economically, politically, and cultur-ally. He dismissed as economically irrational the jobs, sales, and the very continuation of France's industries that depended on protected colonial sources and markets where, after all, profits were made. The benefits of empire can be difficult to quantify. But the expense that the colonial added to the state budget was more than made up by taxing indigenous people with forced labor for the costs of colonial rule and pacification. From the empire or dependencies came increased flows of resources, like Algerian oil and New Caledonian nickel.[44] Add to the account the brisk sales of French weaponry to the new national armies, as well as the millions of much-needed low-waged immigrant workers.

Consider the soldiers recruited from the colonies. They served as mostly supporting troops in World War I, freeing metropolitan soldiers for combat. But half the Free French soldiers who landed in Provence in the summer of 1944 were from North and West Africa. The defend-ers of Dien Bien Phu in 1954 Indochina were largely North African soldiers. Then, also in the postwar, there arrived the millions of indus-trial and service workers from the colonies—called "immigrant work-ers" after their homelands declared their independence from France—who proved so important for French growth, world status, and cultural benefits. Marseille treats these benefits to France as externalities, that is, he did not count them in the balance sheet of empire. In this strange, but not acknowledged, way, the French economic miracle of the post-war years was one of most valuable gifts given by the peoples of the former colonies to France. With this study, Marseille reinforced his readers' own desires that they should go on to happy new lives in a modern capitalist France, once (seemingly) divorced from the old en-cumbrance of Greater France.

General Charles de Gaulle was chagrined by the loss of grandeur he feared a shrunken France would suffer. But he refused to make the only peace possible that would keep Algeria politically connected to France: extending full French citizenship to the Arab and Berber populations, and so seating a hundred North African deputies in the metropole's legislature, there to take part in deciding the fate of the European nation. With Algerian oil, for example, still arriving in France, if per-haps at a bit higher price—and no Algerian war to wage—decoloniza-tion galvanized the growth of the modern hi-tech industries of which the nation is rightly proud. So, decolonization, although it destroyed the Fourth Republic and brought de Gaulle to power via a military coup d'état, caused few economic complaints. Good riddance; a divorce after a bad marriage, the partners turning their backs on the past to get on with new lives.

But the colonial divorce and with it the new French social modernity killed aesthetic modernism. Much of the empire had chosen independence. And since the end of empire, France has ceased to be the creative center of the West.[45] It took a little time for the news of the death of modernism to get out. France's capital holdings in the form were extensive. There is no denying the glories of a mannerist late modern in the works of Samuel Beckett and Jean Genet in literature, in Pierre Boulez's musical experiments with the twelve-tone system and with electronic sound, in the sculptures of César Baldaccini (usually referred to by just his first name) in the paintings of the aged Picasso, and, in film, in the Nouvelle Vague. In fact, during the Algerian war, we saw some of the finest modernist work produced in France with Genet's antiwar plays.

Since France got the news of the end of modernism first, French intellectuals had an earlier opportunity to meditate on this loss and its aftermath. We owe to the French intellectuals active in the 1970s and 1980s the best descriptions of the dawning of postmodernity. Lyotard, Roland Barthes, Foucault, and of course Jacques Derrida delivered the message. Derrida was born and spent his youth in Algeria; Foucault lived some years in North Africa;[46] but one will search in vain through the works of these provisioners of our "French theory" for any serious engagement with France's colonial past.[47] The moment of the French modern passed with the end of empire, but because of the heavy cultural air congestion in those decades, the flight of the owl of Minerva was delayed.

I think we can see the turning point best in art. Compare the blockbuster show, "Primitivism" in Twentieth Century Art, organized by William Rubin in 1984 at the Museum of Modern Art (MoMA) in New York and Jean-Hubert Martin's immense 1989 exhibition, Magiciens de la Terre (Magicians of the Earth), installed at the Centre Pompidou and in the renovated former meat-packing sheds of La Villette in Paris. The New York show was everything that people who cared about the arts of the so-called third world scorned: "primitive" art shown in prettified, noncontextualized, unhistorical, formalist, and culturally ignorant displays. The MoMA show was all about how great Western artists had appropriated visual ideas from the art (no artists, just the art) of the third world, and nothing about the ex-colonial world, peoples, and artists from where and whom the art came. It marked the apogee of the classic modernist tradition of Western primitivism; in representation and catalogue, William Rubin firmly and confidently linked the art of the colonized to twentieth-century aesthetic modernism.[48]

In the mid-1980s, such a show could only have been conceived in the United States. During the years of the cold war, some of our intellectuals had persuaded themselves that not only were our hands clean of imperial expansion but that we—the new United States of the eighteenth century—ourselves had been the "first new nation," and are still therefore a worthwhile model for the third world to follow.[49] A year later, in reaction to the MoMA show, Jean-Hubert Martin, director of the Paris Biennale, imagined doing things in a radically different way. Instead of putting on the usual exhibitions of up-and-coming young Western artists—as André Malraux had originally conceived the Biennale when in the 1960s France wanted to take back the leadership of modernism from New York—Martin aimed at questioning, for the arts, the existing rapports between the so-called center and the so-called periphery. He intended "to treat contemporary art production from a global, worldwide scale."[50]

When the new-model Biennale opened in May 1989, works by fifty Western artists went on display at the art museum of the Centre Pompidou of which Martin had become the director in 1988. Meanwhile, the vast glass and wrought-iron galleries at La Villette showed often very large installations by fifty artists from Asia, Africa, and Latin America. For Martin, the 1931 Colonial Exposition served as "a negative reference point." In his exhibition he wanted to "break the borders that modernity has erected to protect itself." If in 1984 formalist principles guided Rubin's selection and exhibition style in New York, to Martin it seemed important "to emphasize the functional rather than the formal aspects of that spirituality [of third world art]." Consulting with anthropologists knowledgeable about the societies from which the art came, in Magiciens de la Terre, Martin wanted to reconnect art and society by evoking the pieces' auras and by honoring the artists—no matter from where—who made them.[51]

The show proved a disappointment. It had been very expensive to organize and not many people came, at least not to La Villette. The *post*modern breakout seemed to have failed, at least that time. In 2002 Martin, now director of the Düsseldorf Museum Kunst Palast tried again with Art That Heals, an international show of the works of artist-healers: a Navajo healer—sand painter, a Chinese woman artist living in New York who remained connected to traditional medicines, and two Ethiopian scholar-artists whose talismanic paintings were meant to cure. The show toured widely but not to very large publics.

The French modern began with the conquest of the colonial empire. The colonies became major centers of modernist experiments in architecture, city planning, public health, and, of course, the arts.[52] Postmodernity began with the dissolution of the colonial empire. The abstract, non-Western Other of mystery and magic in the art of Paul Gaugin, Picasso, and the surrealists had suddenly become visible in the postwar years as flesh-and-blood fellow humans—sometimes with weapons in hand—demanding recognition and the independence of real people living exploited lives. Both the belief in universal rules and in a world made of formal arts elements could not assimilate these assertive, once misrecognized but always there, newcomers.[53]

Another thing united the purely aesthetic with the new colonial project. To escape from the two poles of realism and bourgeois art in the mid-century aesthetic field, Gustave Flaubert for the novel, Édouard Manet for painting, and Baudelaire for poetry proclaimed a radical split of art from morality. Henceforth art would not be about society or injustice or manners, but about art itself.[54] The escape of both Baudelaire and Flaubert, relatively unharmed, from legal prosecutions for having written indecent works is proof not of the power of bourgeois moralism, but of a growing acceptance among even the most conventional that the aesthetic and the moral could be separable.

Both modernism and colonialism were driven by a cult of newness, by attempts to sound the dark reaches of the heart, by a search for new forms, a desire to experiment, and the urge for adventure. Of course, both artists and colonizers desired to escape the tyranny of the new market society. Rimbaud gave up invention in poetry writing for the thrill of personal imperial adventures. The gunrunning that he did both for income and excitement—to take a distinction from Karl Polanyi—involved him only in buying and selling, not in the market system of capitalism.[55]

Going beyond exhausted older art was the formal reason for the turn to modernism; the escape from history was the societal impulse behind aesthetic modernism. That is why both so many artists and their middle-class appreciators embraced it. In later nineteenth-century France, new families with new money bought the impressionist paintings, and their sensitive and financially dependent children were enthralled by the will to freedom of Baudelaire and Rimbaud. The other great newness of the imagination was the colonial empire. Here lived people without history, people who had always been primitive and, compared to decadent and capitalist France, would—hopefully—remain primitive. In the colonies carefully handcrafted arts still ruled; individual artists produced beautiful things admired by all. The storyteller was honored; he told tales to appreciative auditors who valued them far above the everyday things of material life. As Andrea Fabry has pointed out in the context of Central European imperial cultures, "the modernist artwork demands of the reader ample time, concentration, and undivided attention that only a certain socioeconomic class can afford." If, as I am proposing, we substitute for "socialeconomic class" the word "tribe," we can see the continuing appeal, the affinity, of the colonial world to struggling modernist artists.[56]

Important modernist artists hated the European admixtures to colonial lives. They painted it out. Gauguin, Auguste Renoir, or Matisse, like Marshal Louis-Hubert Lyautey, preferred an imagined pure undiluted original culture.[57] The real was permanent and out of time; a colonial platonism defined modernist ontology. These were peoples whose art could enrich ongoing experiments with form and color. We see here a meeting of the art of empire and the empire of art.[58]

France will have another chance to declare the end to the modernism-colonialism nexus when in 2006 the museum of African, Amerindian, Asian, and Pacific arts, the Musée du Quai Branly, is scheduled to open. Stéphane Martin, its director, sees the relocation of these works —collected in the days of colonialism—to Jean Nouvel's elegantly modern building on Quai Branly as the marker of the end of France's colonial era.[59] Let's all go to see if this is so.

5

JOHN LOCKE,

IMPERIALISM, AND THE FIRST

STAGE OF CAPITALISM

John Locke was the greatest insurance agent in the history of capital-ism. He added what we might call the "American clause" to the health insurance policy of modern capitalism. "In the beginning all the World was America," he wrote in the "Second Treatise of Government," thereby offering Europe's new colonial possessions as the guarantee of the future stability of the social system back home.[1] Locke's interest in the New World extended beyond the philosophical discussion of the "Second Treatise." He also avidly collected and devoured books of great voyages and explorations. Through his patron Anthony Ashley Cooper, the first earl of Shaftesbury, he became proprietor of thou-sands of acres of undeveloped land in the province of Carolina, as well as a member of a number of companies created to profit from the overseas lands. He served on governmental bodies instituted to oversee the colonial empire. A significant portion of his income came to him from his work as a colonial civil servant and from his investments in the colonies. His life was intimately tied up with America, the West Indies, and India. And so was his thought. Locke employed the vast unex-ploited resources of the New World to supply the key premise that lay at the foundation of the argument of his political philosophy. In his "Second Treatise" he summoned up the New World to validate the society emerging in the old. As the first philosopher of the emergent world system,[2] he deserves, at the very least, a statue in front of the World Bank.[3]

Taking up Quentin Skinner's welcome challenge, if not the exaggerated historicism of the Cambridge School, this essay will pursue "the possibility of a dialogue between philosophical discussion and historical evidence."[4] It will first outline Locke's justifications for the existence of private property as he put them forth in his "Second Treatise." It will then demonstrate the logical inadequacy of these arguments, as well as their irrelevance to English society both at the moment of the composition of the treatise and at that of its publication. Finally, it will extract the subtle argument Locke wove into the discussion of the "Second Treatise." For its coherence depended on an aporia: the existence of land for the taking in the New World. By uncovering his unstated assumption of the availability of infinite resources, we may transcend both the factual and logical errors, which a historically naive reading of his text reveals, and rightly adjudge Locke to be the wise organic intellectual both of the seventeenth-century British elite and of future generations of capitalist ruling classes.[5]

Locke's explanation of the origins of the commonwealth and of private property in his "Second Treatise of Government" is so full of sweet reasonableness that finding fault with it borders on churlishness. And yet Locke's argument is vulnerable. Like his predecessors Hugo Grotius, Samuel von Pufendorf, and Thomas Hobbes, he started his analysis of human society from the notion that humankind once lived in a state of nature: "'Tis often asked as a mighty Objection, where are, or ever were, there any Men in such a State of Nature?"[6] Unlike other thinkers who began their discussions of the origins of society by positing a hypothetical state of nature, Locke granted historical, and indeed current, reality to that state. He offered as evidence of his claim two examples from contemporary life. To this day, he argued, nations, and therefore their rulers, dwell in a state of nature one with another. Moreover, "The Promises and Bargains for Truck, etc. between the two Men in the Desert Island mentioned by Garcilasso De la Vega, in his History of Peru, or between a Swiss and an Indian, in the Woods of America are binding to them, though they are perfectly in a State of Nature, in reference to one another."[7]

According to Locke, both "natural Reason which tells us that Men, being once born, have a right to their Preservation," and revelation, which gives us an account of God's providing "the Earth to the Children of Men, giv[ing] it to Mankind in common," substantiate an original state of common ownership of the things of this earth.[8] But the same God who "hath given the World to Men in common, hath also given them reason to make use of it to the best advantage of Life, and convenience."[9] And yet to give the earth to all mankind and not provide for its appropriation and undisputed use by any particular man would be unreasonable on God's part, and Locke's God was an especially reasonable—one might say, an accommodating—Enlightenment personage. Here too, at a key point in his argument, Locke took his evidence from the New World: "The Fruit or Venison, which nourishes the wild Indian, who knows no Inclosure, and is still a Tenant in common, must be his, and so his, i.e. a part of him, that another can no longer have any right to it, before it can do him any good for the support of his Life."[10] Locke could then offer his famous formulation that, if "the Earth, and all inferior Creatures be common to all Men, [and] yet every Man has a Property in his own Person," it followed that "whatsoever that he removes out of the state that Nature hath provided, and left it in, he hath mixed his Labour with, and joyned to it something that is his own, and thereby makes it his property."[11]

Two important observations are in order here. First, this act did not require the common consent of the rest of mankind, for we would have starved long ago had we been obliged to await this sanction on our survival.[12] Second, Locke did not differentiate between our own labor and that of our living chattels and employees: "Thus the Grass my Horse has bit; the Turfs my Servant has cut; and the Ore I have digg'd in any place where I have a right to them in common with others, becomes my Property, without the assignation or consent of any body."[13] Despite his location of its origins in the state of nature, Locke wrote about property in what was for the seventeenth century the most modern of contexts, namely, property as capital—"my Horse"—as embodied in hired labor—"my Servant"—and as resources—"the Ore I have digg'd."

At this juncture of the argument, Locke again turned to the New World with evidence of the practice of people still in the state of nature. "This Law of reason," he explained, "makes the Deer, that Indian's who hath killed it; 'tis allowed to be his goods who hath bestowed his labour upon it, though before, it was the common right of every one." And then to connect the life of the primitive Indian with that of the contemporary Englishman, and thus the Old World with the new, he added that "amongst those who are counted the Civiliz'd part of Mankind . . . this original Law of Nature for the beginning of Property, in what was before common, still takes place" in respect to the fruits of the efforts of fishermen and hunters."[14]

Why does Locke draw his examples almost indifferently at one moment from the most modern capitalist society and at the next moment from the life of the first inhabitants of America? Was he employing what would become the not uncommon Enlightenment strategy of framing arguments to speak of all of humankind, to articulate a natural law of society as true in the time of Adam and Eve as now; as valid for English landowners, merchants, and their employees as for the natives of Jamaica, the Carolinas, and Africa? Certainly this must have been one of his motives, but only one. However, we must see where his doctrine of the origins and rights of property led him before we are in a position to assess the full import of Locke's pervasive exoticism. To this end, we must now turn to the limits that Locke set—and then overcame—to the appropriation of the possessions of God's earth.

Locke argued that the same divinely given law of nature that allows us to own things necessary for our survival by mixing our labor with them "does also bound the use of that Property too." We are given the things of this earth to enjoy "as much as anyone can make use of to any advantage of life before it spoils." But, he wrote empathetically, "Nothing was made by God for Man to spoil or destroy." Moreover, the new owner of land, for example, cannot claim all for himself; there must remain "enough, and as good," with which others may mix their labor.[15] Voicing moral qualms of this sort seems scarcely the work of a great apologist for the economically most rapacious part of the population of the seventeenth century. Peter Laslett has, I think, correctly questioned whether such moral scruples would have deterred a man who was simply "the spokesman of a rising class, the middle class, the capitalists, the bourgeoisie."[16] As we shall see, Locke was both much more and much less than what those simple-recipe words describe.

Locke did need to provide a means for relaxing the stern Calvinist injunctions not to waste or misuse in order to preserve the principle of equal access to resources. But the realities of seventeenth-century English commercial society were not so easily overcome. The commercial society of the day was a given that no sensible man could gainsay. But the strong principles of equity governing property—what E. P. Thompson called the "moral economy"—was also very much alive in the popular spirit. Neither governments nor political thinkers of the age dared take the grave risk to ignore it.

The means Locke hit on was, in his quaint phrase, "a little piece of yellow metal." He argued:

"It is plain that Men have agreed to disproportionate and unequal Possession of the Earth, they have by a tacit and voluntary consent found out a way, how a man may fairly possess more land than he himself can use the product of, by receiving in exchange for the overplus, Gold and Silver, which may be hoarded up without injury to any one, these metalls not spoileing or decaying in the hands of the Possessor."[17] Although it may strike some that the suspension of injunctions grounded in natural law by the provision of a few gold and silver coins is an unseemly, not to say inelegant, solution to a philosophical problem—on the order of René Descartes's use of the pineal gland to solve the mind-body problem he had created for himself—this infelicity is not the chief problem with Locke's argument. Rather, his greatest difficulties grew from his uses of *consent*, that most delicate and most explosive issue of seventeenth-century political life and political philosophy.

Locke was intent on basing his doctrine of the right to property on a notion of property-for-survival, a version of a labor theory of value. He eschewed the positions taken by Grotius and Pufendorf, both of whose analyses of the origins of property he knew well, for they based the right of property on the concurrence of the rest of humankind. And throughout the "Second Treatise," Locke held fast to his refusal to rest the right of exclusive ownership on the consent of one's fellows.[18] How then could he argue that the great act of suspending the limits on the acquisition of possessions set by a God-given natural law might be accomplished by "a tacit and voluntary consent" of men in society?[19] How could a law of nature be suspended by human agreement? If this were so, men could compact—if they could fashion a majority—to make of the commonwealth a democracy of the rabble and then vote to take away the property of the possessors. Such was neither an idle nor an unheard-of fear. The issue of who might properly and safely participate in the political leadership of the nation had not been laid to rest in the course of the Puritan Revolution, which had adjourned only in 1660. It made up one of the grievances of the parliament against the restored monarchy. A second revolution, in 1688, was named "Glorious" in no small degree because the big property owners of Britain had their rights confirmed as a result. Locke had been working on the problem of property and government well before 1688. Resolving just this issue, once and for all, in no small degree determined the strategies of argument he employed in the *Two Treatises.* Rather than being an apologist for the Glorious Revolution, Locke had thought it before it happened.[20]

We are used to encountering these sorts of blatant inconsistencies in Locke. That all our ideas originate in experience, as he asserted in the *Essay Concerning Human Understanding,* except the idea of God, whose existence we can deduce, is only the most famous.[21] We have been accustomed to forgiving Locke his philosophical errors because his sense of reality, his metaphysical and political savvy, was so keen. We honor him in the history of philosophy as the outstanding English representative of Cartesian good sense, unlike his more brilliant empiricist predecessor Hobbes, whose rigor led him to frame a logic of tyranny, or his heir Bishop George Berkeley, whose unrelenting empiricism required him to commend our experienced ideas to God's mind when they were not being thought by us. However, even if we allowed Locke his coin trick as the way individuals might own more than they could cultivate, store, or consume, we would have to forgive him further lapses of logic. If Locke's main concern had been purely the divine and human abhorrence of spoilage and waste, he would not have had to provide a money economy, at least not from the point of view of philosophical argumentation, to avoid this violation of natural law. Barter was practiced by many of the peoples about whom Locke read in his books of voyages and travel. Moreover, one can store valuable things available in excess of needs in many forms other than gold and silver coins. Ingots of iron, carved stones, art, elegant clothing, and utensils have all been employed by various peoples to store unconsumed wealth; nor did these repositories of social surplus serve as means of exchange in any modern sense. To display their opulence and thus gain greater status, families in certain New World cultures, for example, the sophisticated inhabitants of the northwest coast of North America, held great potlatch ceremonies, which amazed European visitors because of the splendor and volume of treasure given away or consumed. Naturally, competing families had to reciprocate, and thereby the exchange of goods and services was facilitated among a scattered and warlike people. More than most contemporaries, Locke knew the many ways other cultures solved their version of the spoilage and exchange problem. A more important point is that even if we were to take Locke's point that accumulated coins liberate us from our moral qualms about keeping barns full of wheat and root cellars overflowing with rotting crops, we would not thereby be freed from the other limit imposed on us by natural law. The storage of wealth in the form of money does not leave "enough, and as good" so that others might live. Locke's theory of property violates this second limit set by a natural law the validity of which Locke never questioned or claimed suspended.

Was Locke then simply a hopelessly muddled ideologue of the new breed of men of wealth like his patron and investment advisor Shaftesbury? The answer, I believe, is no. In his justification for private property, and for differences in wealth, Locke made a philosophical move that in its seeming illogicality puts in relief the substance of his lasting contribution to appeasing the sense of injustice on the part of the propertyless in a society ruled by owners. The problem lies with Locke's paradox of property. After the experience of civil war followed by continuing conflict over authority in the state, Locke's proposal of property as the basis of public order in the commonwealth was at once an astute insight into the deeper meaning of the troubles of his century and prescient advice for future rulers and legislators charged with rendering societies immune to periodic outbreaks of revolutionary fevers. Writing of the limits on the Supreme Power in the commonwealth, the doctor turned policy advisor prescribed the cure for popular revolution: "For the preservation of Property being the end of Government, and that for which Men enter into Society, it necessarily supposes and requires, *that the People should have Property*, without which they must be suppos'd to lose that by entring into Society, which was the end for which they entered into it."[22] The social and economic setting in which Locke wrote the "Second Treatise"—a conjuncture of intensified development of the nation's land, now overwhelmingly in the hands of private owners, with a large landless population of poorly paid laborers and masterless men—renders paradoxical a theory of property whereby one simply mixed labor with unimproved land and became the owner of the parcel, and thereafter a person presumably devoted to the continuing good order of the realm. For in late seventeenth-century England, what meaning could be attached to the injunction that we are obliged to leave "enough, and as good" for others? In the sense in which Locke understood the word, not many people in his day possessed property, that is, land in freehold.[23] Locke did not innocently observe the world from an ivory tower. Neither his public service nor his business connections could have left him unmindful of the absolute shortage of land in England in his own day.

But there was land, quite enough and very good, in the New World. Locke, better than most men in public life of late-seventeenth-century England, knew this too. It must be emphasized that in his own day he was credited with being one of the most knowledgeable of Englishmen about the colonial world. He came by this knowledge in several ways. Locke was tied to this New World by the three most powerfully binding forces of his life. First, his imagination was excited by the poorly mapped and little known places across the seas. He loved to read books of travel, geography, and explorations. From them he gained an extensive knowledge of what was known of the new overseas lands coming into the European consciousness.[24] Second, his economic well-being depended in part on his investments in various colonial ventures. The Earl of Shaftesbury, a principal investor in the company, had Locke named to the new office of secretary to the Lords Proprietors of Carolina.[25] His friend put him onto investments with the Bahamas Adventurers (another undertaking of the Lords Proprietors), Richard Thompson's Company, the Royal Africa Company, and the East India Company.[26] On the eve of his retirement, as much as half of Locke's living was drawn from these investments.[27] Third, his career in public service brought him his practical knowledge of colonial matters and much of the rest of his income. Locke spent his two terms in state service helping to fashion and direct imperial colonial policy. From 1673 to 1675, while he served the Lords Proprietors of Carolina, he obtained, through Shaftesbury, a parallel post with the Council of Trade and Plantations.[28] In 1675, the Earl of Danby, the new minister of Charles II and an enemy of Shaftesbury, dissolved the council. Only some years after the Glorious Revolution and Locke's return from the continent was it recreated. From 1696 to his retirement in 1700 he served on its successor that William III had had reconstituted as the Board of Trade.[29]

Thus a theoretical aporia filled in by practice pointed Locke toward the solution of his problem. If in the beginning the whole world was America, Locke understood that in the late seventeenth century, a great part of it still remained in the circumstances he defined as the state of nature. In the "Second Treatise" he wrote of "the first Ages of the World, when Men were more in danger to be lost, by wandering from their Company, in the then vast Wilderness of the Earth, than to be straitned from want of room to plant in."[30] But such vastness still existed, for he continued:

> And the same measure may be allowed still, without prejudice to any body, as full as the World seems. For supposing a Man, or Family, in the state they were, at first peopling of the World by the Children of Adam, or Noah; let him plant in some in-land, vacant places of America, we shall find that the Possessions he could make himself upon the measures we have given, would not be very large, nor, even to this day, prejudice the rest of Mankind, or give them reason to complain, or think themselves injured by this Man's Incroachment, though the race of Men have now spread themselves to all corners of the World, and do infinitely exceed the small number [which] was at the beginning.[31]

Locke here was offering the New World, specifically the colonial settlements of America, as validation of his sociopolitical philosophy. For "even to this day" one could go there, and taking neither too much nor denying another his share, mix one's labor with the meadows and forests to join the ranks of England's proprietors. If one possessed neither adequate land nor gold and silver money in England, as were the circumstances of the vast majority of the nation, Locke offered America as the key that would give access to participation in the life of the commonwealth.

But wait, what of the aboriginal inhabitants of these lands, the Indians, for example? Were they not the owners of the land even before the first vessel had embarked from Europe? Locke offered two arguments for why European settlers had the right to take possession of these supposedly new lands. First, although he granted that indeed God had given the world to men in common, he reminded the reader that "he gave it them for their benefit, and the greatest Conveniences of Life they were capable to draw from it." Therefore, "it cannot be supposed he meant it should remain common and uncultivated. He gave it to the use of the Industrious and Rational, (and Labour was his title to it)."[32] Accordingly, to obtain the right to a part of nature a person must not simply mix his labor with it, he is obliged to maximize the productivity of the effort. As Locke wrote, "If either the Grass of his Inclosure rotted on the Ground, or the Fruit of his planting perished without gathering, and laying up, this part of the Earth, notwithstanding his Inclosure, was still to be looked on as Waste, and might be the Possession of any other."[33] With this philosophical tour de force Locke managed with the same argument both to justify the dispossession of the ancestral lands of the Indians in distant America and the ongoing enclosure of the commons once set aside by custom for the use of the peasants of the English countryside.

Locke's double-duty argument gives us further encouragement to accept the correctness of reading him as a great philosopher of the developing world system linking the Old World with the New with ties of domination and subordination. Clearly, by both the prime measure—that of human energy expended to modify nature—and, for Locke, the necessary correlative—that of the maximization of production—most Amerindians failed to meet the principal qualifications for owning a part of America. In addition, Europeans were warranted to displace the original inhabitants of Europe's overseas colonies because the natives of these regions did not use money as a means of exchange. Locke reasoned, "There are still great Tracts of Ground to be found, which (the Inhabitants thereof not having joyned with the rest of Mankind, in the consent of the Use of their common Money) lie waste, and are more than the people, who dwell on it, do, or can make use of, and so still lie in common."[34] Locke granted that certain Indians used artifacts known as *wampompeke* (wampum), which he understood to perform some of the functions of money. But here his ethnographic reading proved a great aid to the validation of the uneven exchange in the world system. He understood that *wampompeke* was used in ceremonial situations to mark treaties agreed to or transactions completed. It was not meant as a means of commercial exchange ("common Money") in the sense that coins of precious metal were in Europe. Accordingly, the aboriginal inhabitants of America on this count, too, continued in the state of nature. The lands that the Amerindians hunted and even farmed were not theirs as the rents from Locke's estate in Somerset were his, even while he lived in Oxford, or London, or in continental exile.[35]

Locke, even more than we have hitherto realized, understood the driving forces of his age. He clearly spelled out the relation of property, colonial expansion, and good government. Property as the criterion for participation in the political life of the country, property as a guarantee of conservative demeanor, the promise of property as an inducement for social tranquility—these were the key functions Locke assigned to the ownership of resources in the "Second Treatise." One had but to mix one's labor with the bounty of God's nature to create this property. Locke's political writings—however much aimed at contemporary issues—sought to lay a sound foundation for a theory of government that would both satisfy the elite and placate the governed of the day, and beyond this, hold the loyalties of future generations.[36]

Commentators have noted the curious ambiguity of Locke's political writings which permitted him to endorse the actions of the energetically rapacious men of wealth of his and later ages and at the same time hold forth a promise of unprecedented political participation for the many.[37] This ambiguity works in a number of ways. Readers of the "Second Treatise" quickly note the slippage between "property" and "life, liberty, and Property," as if they were the same concept. But by so tying life and liberty to property, he excluded the vast bulk of the people from government. Again, in his *Letters Concerning Toleration*, Locke described the government that followed the state of nature as one which should see to "the peace, riches, and public commodities of the whole people,"[38] and not one, as we might expect from knowing the argument of the "Second Treatise," which catered only to the needs of the property owners. Moreover, no age that had seen both great bands of ideologically aroused and armed men call to account their king and numbers of newly monied men find their way to the top could easily accept a political theory that envisioned rule by an absolute monarch or a closed political elite. We may understand Locke's own attack on Sir Robert Filmer's defense of absolute rule in the "First Treatise" as evidence on this point. And yet that coalition of aristocrats and new men with whom Locke moved was not yet prepared to open the door to power so that the strata below them in wealth and eminence might enter.

C. B. Macpherson proposed a way he believed Locke resolved this ambiguity. In Macpherson's view, Locke's doctrine of the right of exclusive possession created by adding one's labor to resources pointed the way both to the modern capitalist notion of private property and, by implication, to a contemporary theory of political participation.[39] However, as we have seen, in terms both of the unresolved tensions of seventeenth-century life and, more important, of Locke's estimate of future developments, this offers no solution at all. There simply did not exist in Locke's England enough unclaimed land, mines, or forests with which a rapidly growing landless majority of the population might mix its labor. In Locke's lifetime Dutch engineers were being hired in Britain to push back the sea so as to gain a little more precious land. As we have also seen, his doctrine of money involved Locke in hopeless muddles and blatant violations of natural law.

In the late 1690s when his experiences on the Board of Trade had brought him once more into direct connection with the workings of empire, and perhaps when he had meditated some on the implications of the arguments he had advanced in the "Second Treatise," he added to the existing version of the text the judgment "that the increase of lands and the right imploying of them is the great art of government."[40] Locke's own insight that the solution to his philosophical problem of how to ground a theory of a dynamically stable social order lay just across the Atlantic now stands out in its full, if ominous, clarity. Going well beyond the simplistic social theories of the mercantilists of his day, his political philosophy integrated the reality of colonialism and the beckoning riches of colonial resources into modern political philosophy in a new way. He made the colonial empire a vital bond between Britain's new elite and those they governed. He thereby strengthened the nascent liberalism of British society by building into it the promise of growth, of more for all, of social peace through empire. Moreover, understanding his idea of empire in this way suggests the direction for a reassessment of those theories of modern imperialism—Lenin's included—that see such expansion as a "last stage," rather than as a constitutive element of the liberal tradition.

In the history of philosophy Locke's use of a whole continent, indeed, several continents, as a deus ex machina for his philosophical system is unprecedented. But then again the violent expansion of the domination of European societies over the rest of the world—a process in its infancy in Locke's day—is also unprecedented. Three hundred years later we can still learn from Locke. For his comprehension of the relation between the Old and the New worlds, however imperfect it may have been, has deepened our own understanding of important currents of thought and of their correlative praxis that, from their early modern beginnings, put the most powerful Western societies on the road to enhancing their power and buttressing their internal stability by appropriating the labor of the people and resources of distant ancient cultures baptized by the minions of European civilization as an empty New World.

6

WHY, SUDDENLY,

ARE THE AMERICANS DOING

CULTURAL HISTORY?

Some years ago a French journal asked me to write a piece on what was new in American history writing. At that moment—the mid-1990s—U.S. historians, especially the young and those specializing in the study of Europe, were turning in growing numbers to the study of cultural history. This is cultural history in the sense of the study both of how people live and of what they create and value. After some reflection, I hit on at least four major reasons for the emergence of a new paradigm.

First, we see change in historical studies because there is a growing sense—in the United States, at least—of the bankruptcy of classical political and diplomatic history writing and of the diminishing returns from the positivist varieties of social history. Criticism of the methodological naïveté, especially of social history with its cult of experience and its working-class essentialism, played a role in the turn to a new cultural history. Feminists questioned the archival fetishism of studies that always found the evidence of male power that men of power had stored there. Second, we are now interested in the hopes and struggles of greater segments of humanity than the (mostly male) members of the working class in Western societies. With women's history, gender history, and, my own interest, imperial history, we have widened our historical focus. New subjects require new methods. The turn to cultural history is of a piece with the emergence of the postcolonial episteme. So, third, we are asking questions that require us to learn the historical meaning and workings of images, gestures, and symbols; of the nonrational and the *non-dit*, the unsaid. To go beyond classic historical positivism, we have had to learn from the other fields where such analyses have been worked out and refined. This new cultural history crosses borders that in the past have been better defended against penetration than those, for example, guarded by the border guards on both sides in the days before the fall of the Berlin Wall. Seeking new insights, we have crossed and recrossed the old frontiers of the established disciplines of history, literary studies, philosophy, anthropology, art history—to name the most important. By means of the new cultural history we are better able also to cross the frontiers of states and ethnicities to regain a view of a whole, if diverse, humanity as our final subject of study. If we are to write good history in an age of globalization, we too must broaden our own horizon. But a final reason, more important than considerations of method, is a political one: cultural history is the last—or, at least, the current—version of a project for liberation that originated in Western Marxism in the 1960s. It takes up the torch from the social historians of the 1970s and 1980s. It can be understood as a continuation of that contestatory and emancipatory project by other means.

Western Marxism, which—differing somewhat from both Georg Lukács's and Maurice Merleau-Ponty's understanding of the term— Perry Anderson described in his book *Considerations on Western Marxism*, groups various European projects for revitalizing the Marxian legacy and fitting it to the possibilities of progressive movements of Western societies that did not, would not, look to the Soviet Union as the model for all socialisms. It rejected base-superstructural formulations. Eschewing economic issues, it reformulated the labor theory of value as a moral claim. Departing from the scientistic discourse of both the Second and Third Internationals, it worked broadly in the German idealist tradition, that is, in the wake of G. W. F. Hegel or Immanuel Kant. Western Marxism looked for a historical praxis that would bring liberation even if the Western proletariat seemed increasingly unable to fulfill its historic mission of uniting itself with philosophy to make the revolution. Giving up Friedrich Engels, Karl Johan Kautsky, and, finally, Lenin—all of whom privileged the so-called objective conditions for revolution—this new Marxism turned to the exploration of consciousness as the arena in which the proletariat's will to act was subverted or misled by the cultural apparatus of advanced capitalism. Major schools of Western Marxism, each in their own way—the Gramscians, members of the Frankfurt School—tried to revitalize a dialectical, consciousness-centered reading of how capitalism might be rejected and workers returned to the path Marxist philosophy marked out for them.

In history writing in the United States and Britain, where these theorists were studied by young historians looking to contribute in their work to the project of liberation, the publication of E. P. Thompson's *The Making of the English Working Class* (1963) and his active work from 1959 to 1963 with the *New Left Review* launched an important new initiative. In the work of Thompson we found a vision of a working class as, not that of an object formed and arrayed against class enemies, but rather as a historical subject in the process of coming into being. Written after his break with the British Communist Party over the 1956 Russian invasion of Hungary, Thompson offered us a working-class history with Lenin, that is, vanguardism, left out. In his elegantly written story of the rise of an English labor movement in the decades before Chartism, Thompson tells of workers creating their own historical project without external, that is, bourgeois intellectuals' coming to them bearing the philosophy of the revolution. The enemy of this historical conception was, of course, the work of the nondissident French communist theorist Louis Althusser. This philosopher of science at the École Normale Supérieure reformulated Marxism as a kind of structural matrix, thereby removing both consciousness and agency from human history. In fact, his synchronic rewrite removed history from workers' histories. Rejecting the Hegelian dialectic of conflict, he made Marx a disciple of Spinoza. In the 1970s and 1980s British Marxists fought a bruising—if not always clear-headed—fight that pitted the philosophic abstractions of Althusser against the Gramscian Hegelianism of Thompson.

In the United States Althusser did not have the same early impact among historians. Most progressive U.S. historians welcomed Thompson's book and articles about the moral economy and the invention of capitalist time. He showed us how to focus on workers' lives and values in a deeper way than the old working-class history of congresses, party programs, and great personalities had done even in the best versions, such as Harvey Goldberg's classic biography *The Life of Jean Jaurès* (1962) or Karl Schorske's 1955 study of the split in German social democracy before World War I. Thompson's example encouraged young historians to drop certain topics of classical labor history. His metanarrative of working-class self-creation freed us from worrying about our lack of economic analysis—abandoned by the Frankfurt School after Hitler's coming to power—or the dead-end political theory of Western Marxism—which melded the history of the capitalist state with that of a ubiquitous totalitarianism. Nor did we have to consider employers. As this one-class account conceptualized social history, the bosses were not seen to play any important role either in the lives or the consciousness of workers. Thompson's diffident refusal to write about the Irish, Welsh, and Scottish parts of the British working class was remedied in 1976 by Herbert Gutman in the United States, who wrote brilliantly about the confluence of ethnicity and class in U.S. history and trained a school of American Thompsonians in his own right. It is not clear why neither of these two men wrote about the women workers so important in each of these industrializations. Meanwhile, Eugene Genovese, in studies of the worlds of American Southern planters and that of the slaves, employed Antonio Gramsci's concept of cultural hegemony and counterhegemonic resistance in rich and subtle ways.

In the 1970s and early 1980s the search for a locus or generator of resistance to capitalist hegemony in the lives and values of members of oppressed groups in American society, African Americans, new immigrants, and increasingly women; and in European societies, regions, small towns, trades, came to be called social history. Under the influence of sociologist Charles Tilly and other like-minded researchers such as William Sewell and Joan W. Scott in her first study (1974), young historians, often employing sophisticated statistical procedures, produced monographs on local industries or towns aimed, ultimately, at least in Tilly's case, at a grand project of understanding the state and the workers in nineteenth-century Europe. This early version of American social history was highly empirical, even Lockean, in the breathtakingly direct way it linked events and thoughts.

If revolutionary consciousness was not brought to the workers by a political vanguard, where did their ideas come from? From experience, the workers' own experience, answered the new social historians. In a much-debated article, Joan Scott rejected the naïveté of this approach, which once had been her own: "Experience," she now wrote, "is not the origin of our explanation,"[1] because our experience of the world is mediated by an already extant largely cultural frame. Her piece began not with an example of workers' lives, but, provocatively, rather with the memoirs of a homosexual's coming to consciousness of his non-isolation as a result of the experience of the gay world of public baths. Scott's Kantian reformulation of the world in which we live and work was taken by many Leftist male social historians as the challenge it was meant to be.[2]

In Germany social history also had held sway since the 1960s. The social-historical projects of Hans Ulrich Wehler and of Jürgen Kocka and their associates in the Bielefeld School concentrated on the working class and the state. Each nation's social history differed, of course, and the chief *Problematik* (way of framing questions) in West German scholarship was why, in the years roughly 1870 to 1933, the working class had not managed to make a successful new state. So, in a word, why the Nazis? Both American social historians and this dominant German school were posing parallel questions about why socialism had not come, except, of course, German studies had lots about politics but no place for women, and American studies found it difficult to talk both about workers' lives *and* the state in the same study.

An important aftermath of the antiwar, civil rights, and intra-university struggles of the 1960s in the United States was the displacement of the working class in middle-class intellectuals' imaginations by new social movements such as ecology and anti-nuclear; and those for the rights of women, gays, and African Americans. Where some of the future academics of Students for Democratic Society (SDS) of the late 1960s and early 1970s wanted to see themselves as organic intellectuals of workers needing to be roused, by the 1980s, a spectrum of new social movements, each with its own leadership and agenda, had gained their greater attention and loyalty.

I participated in a researchers' seminar on the international history of the working class held monthly at Columbia University in New York in the 1980s. Attendance shrank through the decade. By the mid-1980s, we had on average only six to ten around the table; we disbanded in 1990. However, the feminist seminar—often meeting in the conference room next door—had a growing following, and many labor historians who were women stopped going to hear papers on male workers in order to explore women's issues. This intellectual change of focus reflected in microcosm the exodus from the young male-dominated and male-led New Left in the mid-1970s of young women intellectuals who wanted to explore ways of ending the hegemony of the male narrative of history. Many wanted to begin writing "herstory."

In 1980 began twelve years of first Reagan and then Bush rule—the first plague, and with it the growing spread of neoconservatism on American intellectual life. This put the Left university on the defensive. More than ever before, theorists replaced the language of economic and political struggle with that of the resistance and of contestation of self-defined social groups. This decisive change—together with the end of hope for China as an alternative socialist model to the flawed and long-abandoned Soviet one—more than anything else set American historiography in search of where and who would bring not radical social change, the possibilities were too limited for such utopian projects, but rather a place of shelter from a world-colossus capitalism. Many of us searched for an arena, however circumscribed, where we might expand freedom; some accepted just the possibilities of transgression, or at least of some gesture of resistance. The 1960s dream of the Marcusean Grand Refusal was gone. The Republicans' antipathy for university intellectuals, and their political as well as budgetary attacks on university research, taught many in the academy a lesson on the connection between principle and self-interest in the scholarly world.

The radical youth of the 1960s had grown up, some of them, to be faculty members in American universities. These were institutions both geographically and ideologically far from the classic proletariat, and they now had students, increasingly ethnically diverse, more interested in finding a place in an American society that did not penalize them for their group identity than in overthrowing it. These researchers, many of whom had gone into history, sociology, philosophy, and literary studies, wanted to move things forward. But how? How might social change come without a powerful, unified historical agent?

For the United States, attention focused first on the women's movement and African Americans. The women's movement had long ago turned from consciousness raising to improving the material conditions of women in employment, public policy, and control of their bodies. The new Religious Right made opposition to the last of these the condition of its support for the Republican regimes. Women were becoming ever more prominent in the historical profession and began implementing their project to write a new historical account: either *her*story as an alternative to *hi*story or, more radically, a history with new categories entirely. From interest in herstory, historians of women moved in the 1980s to a more general appreciation of gender in history. Herstory as much as history ran the risks, some realized, of essentializing women. But gender history, which insisted on the constructed nature of gender relations, could by its methods yield more sophisticated knowledge. The empiricist epistemology of social history made it difficult to adapt it to a new vision of a made-up world. Accordingly, it was often historians of gender who served as pioneers of a new cultural history.[3]

In creating a Rainbow Coalition, with Jesse Jackson as spokesperson, both the veterans and new members of the civil rights movement signaled the passing of an exhausted Black Nationalism. The ecology organizations, changed from the relatively genteel upper middle-class lovers of the outdoors in the 1960s to become mass political formations able to change public policy in the face of devastating government and corporation programs driven by a capitalist instrumental rationality to exploit the resources of American forests, mountains, deserts, and the air we breathe. Meanwhile, in 1969, after a famous confrontation with the New York police at a gay bar in Greenwich Village called the Stonewall—giving its name to the new movement—homosexuals began to organize the political struggle for gay rights and soon afterwards, tragically, for more government attention to the epidemic of AIDS. The grievances of newly self-confident ethnic groups such as the many populations reified under the label *Latinos* began to be heard. In complex ways, Spanish-speaking Americans have made themselves increasingly important in the political process. The Native American peoples movements continue to grow and gain victories such as, most recently, having a Native American museum, controlled by Amerindians, built in two sites—Lower Manhattan and on the Mall in the capital.[4] Can the newest Americans coming from Asia—Indians, Pakistani, Koreans, new Chinese settlers—be far behind in formulating their grievances and staking their claims?

But how could this postmodern mélange be made sense of? If the truth of experience does not enter the eye directly and imprint itself on our brains, how do we form new ideas? The membrane of knowledge, responded some new historians, is culture. Culture gives meaning to language, images, gestures.[5] A conference called in 1989 at Berkeley by Lynn Hunt on the new cultural history and the publication of some of the papers in a volume with that name may mark as good an indicator as any of the emergence of a new group of self-consciously linked cultural historians.

In the first instance, the new cultural historians are partisans of the new social movements. As such, they focus historiographically on the issues that concern members of these movements. These issues, for all their specificity and peculiarity, are universal, global in reach. Following Michel Foucault and Jacques Derrida, the new libratory cultural history universally investigates the right to difference and, especially, ways of deontologizing social categories. For example, the new paradigm has fostered new histories of blackness and whiteness—such as Mathew Frey Jacobson's *Whiteness of a Different Color* or Noel Ignatiev's *How the Irish Became White*—as well as those of diasporas (e.g., Paul Gilroy, *The Black Atlantic*). It tracks down hidden controls and constraints and celebrates resistance and the possibilities of contestation, or at least indeterminacy. Following Foucault, there is interest in understanding how, without passing by way of consciousness, mechanisms of control impinge on the person. These tasks are carried out, above all, by the analysis of language in the broadest sense—discourses, images, gestures. Interest in the lives of workers and ordinary people continues, but now more focused on the politics of everyday life. Sociological *explanation*s continue to coexist, if uneasily, with studies of culturally produced *meanings*.

The model for this switch is cultural anthropology, which has mediated insights from the study of colonized society and itself had learned new lessons from literary criticism. The work of Clifford Geertz of the Princeton Institute for Advanced Study has proven important in adapting literary-textual questions into ones suitable for ethnographic work.

It is important to note that Geertz, too, made his own theoretical turn away from strict Parsonianism so as better to write about Indonesian and Moroccan societies, that is, colonial and postcolonial parts of the world. First at Berkeley and then at Princeton, Natalie Zemon Davis, who has creatively employed the ideas of Geertz, Mikhail Bakhtin, and the *Annales* School in her work on Reformation France, has been very influential in early modern studies. From literary studies there come ways of speaking about difference—women, American blacks, the so-called third world—and about lives on the margins of society—homosexuals, ethnic minorities, immigrants, the insane, the hospitalized, the unsighted, the deaf—all challenges to existing standards and rules. This attack on the canons, the heritages of the powerful, which in literary theory sought the dethronement of great inherited wisdoms and texts of the dead white European males who wrote them, in cultural history seeks to destroy what Eric Hobsbawm continued to champion as "the standard version" of history.[6]

Although such transvaluations ask us to rethink, and deepen our ideas of, what is Left and what is Right in politics, it is not correct a priori to conclude that cultural criticism is less Left than studies of workers' movements. That would border on the hopeful ouvrierism (the dogma endorsing what workers do as always right) of earlier social history. In a contested way, cultural history has set out to complete one aspect of the Enlightenment project—the demystification of the Western world our fathers made. I say in a contested way because the practitioners of the new cultural history divide more or less clearly for or against the Enlightenment. At this writing, in 2005, we cannot say what the outcome of the still raging debate is or will be. The readers of Foucault and, to a lesser degree, of Derrida who thus, consciously or indirectly, take their lessons from Friedrich Nietzsche and Martin Heidegger want to move beyond the European, gendered, and class limitations of Enlightenment values. Hayden White and Dominick LaCapra early worked in this vein. This would also cover many feminist historians, with Joan Scott, now a major shaper of gender studies, at the forefront. The questions investigated by this group tend to explore modes and possibilities of liberation and alterity. Social dominance and limitation is the starting point, and cases of micropolitical resistance or ideological guerilla war, that is, textual deconstruction, constitute the ongoing interest. In their studies they celebrate transgressions and emancipatory ambiguities; they expose phallocratic power and analyze the complex play of sexual politics. Because of its rejection of both totalization and normativity, this school is not likely to offer us a new vision of society. Nor has it shown interest in the long-time problem of the history that focused on process, development, and personality. Rather, it looks at practices, discourses within an inherited, largely taken-for-granted, and ordered—too ordered, it argues—Western world made up of texts. Some of its members even investigate what the old Marxist-oriented historiography saw as progressive moments or events to show their oppressive side: the French Revolution as the moment of women's exclusion from political life, or the (male) labor movement's, or at least its historians,' systematic neglect of women and their work, or the celebration of a humanistic high cultural tradition that thereby masks the white, male, Eurocentric oppression such canons confirm.[7]

The other branch looks more to completing the unfinished Enlightenment project. Many of these historians work in the tradition charted by the Frankfurt School, and especially of its current continuers, Jürgen Habermas in sociology and Lynn Hunt in U.S. French history. Here the agenda is to look at the public sphere as developed in the eighteenth century, and closed in the nineteenth, as a contribution to political liberty, rather than as a tyranny of a few masquerading as the will of the whole to see the dialectical conflict of the life world with the institutions of capitalist society as containing potentials for forging greater freedom in society here and now.[8] I would put the fascinating work of Deirdre McCloskey on the rhetoric of economic discourse here too. We would benefit greatly from her writing more on gender issues in economic theory and rhetoric.

Now this turns out to be a division not only of scholars for and against the implementation of the social rationality of the Enlightenment and the curbing of a triumphant but socially destructive instrumental rationality but it also divides historians who find their theoretical ideas in France from those who look to the tradition of the Frankfurt School. Nietzsche and Heidegger have essentially become naturalized French thinkers; understandably, German history writing has been slow to use their ideas. It also divides thinkers who see the risks to our well-being coming from unleashing the passions and irrationalities of one version of the Nietzschean tradition from those—the ones who start from France—who assume repressive systems of languages, practices, and texts at work that must be disrupted at all cost to permit greater freedom or more choices. In a word, historians who know something of the phenomenon of National Socialism in Germany are not so certain that the greatest threats to human development and freedom were best understood by Nietzsche and Heidegger, or that appeals to the Enlightenment are just an "alibi," in Foucault's scornful dismissal.[9] So the first voice alerting his fellow citizens to the dangers for German democracy of minimizing the importance of the Nazi era in German historiography —the beginnings of the *Historikerstreit*, the historians' conflict—was that of Jürgen Habermas. French studies of the cultural implications of the Vichy years—as distinct from politics, racial policy, and collaboration—after a promising start in the late 1980s (with Christian Faure's *Le projet culturel de Vichy* and Jean-Pierre Rioux's edited volume *Politiques et pratiques culturelles dans la France de Vichy*) seem to have been replaced by a growing interest in the empire.

Perhaps we are beginning to see an end to the curious process of intellectual transmission Peter Schöttler once characterized to me, in the language of the traffic in drugs, as "laundering."[10] That is, taking suspect thinkers from old Germany like Nietzsche, Heidegger, and, most recently, Carl Schmitt, and, like drug dealers attempting to cleanse the traces of the criminal origins of their riches by putting them into legitimate businesses, investing them in French philosophical and historical discourses. So laundered, their ideas can then be sent to American universities as "French theory."[11]

But the division on the Enlightenment overlaps with one on the scope of present-day history writing. Is not the question for or against the *European* Enlightenment largely meaningless outside of its lands of birth or adoption? In a word, we have to ask what our (meaning Western historians) relation is to the researchers and subjects in the greater world outside of Europe and America. We were especially and forcefully challenged on this issue in the aftermath of decolonization. Today the southern hemisphere no longer forms a part of the holdings of the great Western powers, but itself constitutes an important force in world politics. Then, too, the swelling of immigration from Asia, the Caribbean, and South America, especially in the United States and Britain brought the colonial world to the center. Scholars began to occupy posts in the two societies, many themselves originally from once-colonial lands, continue to enrich our understandings with new questions about empire, race, ethnicity, and subaltern culture. With a manifestly globalizing world, even the evil-powerful see postcolonial and global studies as necessary for their own historical practice.[12]

Still, national tunes—especially French and American ones, the two societies I know best—continue to be fiddled while supporters of an alternative globalization and neoliberal business leaders from all over the world set fires over the future socioeconomic development of the planet. Because of the historic nature of Western domination, it is completely understandable that the best historical scholarship done in the nations of the southern hemisphere continues to sketch the foundations of an often essentialist national narrative.[13] Living in the new Rome, we perhaps are situated to see other aspects of how the empire works. To be both coherent and explanatory, histories of all periods will need increasingly to be written with the rest of the known world in mind and in collaboration, or at least in conversation, with historians from the once colonial world.

The inherent interdisciplinarity of cultural history has put historians in touch with creative work in literature, philosophy, art history, anthropology, and if not yet uniting the peoples, at least has done much to unite the scholars of many nations. It is the first history writing that takes seriously the three important aspects of a truth about both contemporary and premodern history: First, in the world before the European nineteenth century, most people lived in richly symbolic worlds relatively untouched by print culture. Second, today we live in a media world, and have done so for some time. For both us and for the people that Columbus encountered, culture as life and culture as representation are identical, or at least nondistinguishable. To be sure, theirs was communal, symbolic, and religious. The complexity is that we live in a world fragmented by a new hyperrealism of TV, film, and electronic communications, while largely the same economically driven forces have, at the same time, and third, opened us to globalized lives. We are subsuming earlier ways of knowing to the dawning global episteme. Yet the research questions most historians continue to pose ignore this great epistemological—and very real—shift. But not entirely. The editors and authors who have collaborated in the review *Public Culture,* for example, early championed and forcefully a cosmopolitan perspective. Work in microhistory, which seeks the general in the study of specific microcosms, is helping establish a new historiography.

Today it is hard to imagine any useful totalizing theory of social life, at least in modern social worlds. There is too much acknowledged heterogeneity for such an effort to be anything but an exercise in religious dogmatisms. With great metanarratives suspect and logical closure impossible, we need an alternative way of studying societies. Pierre Bourdieu's brilliant move away from studying sociological laws to the strategies of groups to evade such controls offers a promising path.[14] Sooner or later, cultural historians will have to confront state power, economic discourses and theoretical claims more systematically. After all, power is also, a little bit, economic, and perhaps legal too. . . .

Power operates, as Foucault has taught us, in often obscure ways. And identity politics, in some cases literary and historical wars over culture, have been the dominant issue, or at least the dominant language, of conflict in American historical scholarship. That is changing, as we have seen, as new studies deconstruct invidious once naturalized identity categories. I hope that in the near future we can create a balance between the pluralism of groups' just claims for justice with a new universalism that links and protects us all, in our shared humanity. And I think many others have made that their project as well.

AFTERWORD

In this moment of neoliberalism when the doctors of economics pre-
scribe ever more and ever freer markets as a kind of lithium for business
cycles, it is important to recall that the harm that empires caused at
home did not stem from their costs or their practice of protectionism.[1]
Today's pervasive economism takes the focus away from the real damage that colonialism caused to democratic forces within a parliamentary framework. And that harm has not been, cannot be, repaired by
more neoliberalism. John Locke first prescribed empire to immunize
an immature and threatened liberal society from the longings of new
have-nots. Since his provision of this pill with poisonous side-effects,
overseas expansion to avoid internal problems has always tempted leaders of parliamentary states with insurgent democracies.

Etienne Balibar has proposed that "rather than always harking back
to the French Revolution and to the real or imagined consequences of
'Jacobinism,'" we should look to more modern times for the origins of
contemporary top-down public policy.[2] Since at least the time of
Charles Baudelaire—or if one prefers political benchmarks—since
Napoleon III's plebescitarian rule, a regime of power was crafted to
contain unruly provincials. Fine-tuned in the Third Republic, it was
sent to the colonies for testing and improvement. And then as needed,
the lessons learned came back to inform the metropolitan order. Since
the nineteenth century overseas expansion and the consequent dialectical movement of knowledge-power between France and the colonies
has increasingly institutionalized the colonial regime inside the nation,
to the point that, today, Balibar speaks of the "introjection of colonial-
ization.[3] Since new cultural forms, new philosophy, new social sciences,
new history writing, new francophone literature, and of course, new

means of control have been worked out in the course of this interactional process of learning, how can we not treat metropoles and colonies as an integrated field of knowledge, as the emergent global episteme? French prisons, mental asylums, and the confessional served Michel Foucault as microcosmic models for trends in really existing societies. But only in areas of the French colonial empire do we see the kind of biopower he described systematically practiced—as governmentality—over large dominated populations. In that sense, too—of improved techniques of social control—is the old claim that empire was a place of experimentation true.[4]

In these chapters I have tried specifically to bring attention to some of the major hidden injuries to modern democratic culture caused by empire. There was, and is, an alternative option available from the beginnings of empire. But it was not taken—or haltingly undertaken— by incipient democratic societies like France, Britain, and the United States. The refusal to extend the "us" to peoples encountered over the course of imperial expansion has delayed democratic inclusion and the growth of *fraternité* at home. The bad consequences of this path not taken have haunted my stories. But why were the new territories or new immigrants from poor lands so regularly constructed as Other by colonial rulers? Because they were strange and far away? Consider France, the peoples of the colonies, and the twentieth-century immigrants from these colonies.

At the height of the French empire a few Europeans ruled often dispersed and hetergeneous peoples mostly of Muslim faith. Exercise of power always begins with naming. In the course of conquering Algeria in the 1830s and 1840s, for example, French state leaders constructed the annexed populations not as future French people but as "Muslims." And this imputed identity was not seen simply as a way of referring to a diverse population by a shorthand religious label; rather, to the builders of empire it meant a total identity.[5] Yet recall that in the eighteenth century the monarchy had made the populations of the coastal communes of Senegal—like the Alsatians, Corsicans, Basques, and Bretons, at about the same time, in fact—subjects of the king.[6] Some of these African French practiced local religions, some were even converted Christians, but the vast majority were Muslims. They led the lives of peasant farmers, traders, pastoralists, and fishermen, with some urban life. Were the lives of backcountry French in the eighteenth century, including not speaking "French," very different from those of the Senegalese?

Remember, too, that with a stroke of the pen, the French Revolution had granted all French Jews full citizenship. That meant the relatively assimilated ones in the southwest, as well as the ghettoized and the dialect-speaking ones in provincial Alsace. Under the monarchy they had been referred to respectively as the "Portuguese nation" and the "German nation." In Paris the different "nations" both mixed and kept separate. Of course among these Jews were believers, nonbelievers, agnostics—all the many shades of religious self-inclusion or opting out. The customs and religious practices of the conquered Arabs, Berbers, and Jews that the French soldiers encountered in newly annexed North Africa could not have been stranger to the French occupiers than those of the most devout of these different continental Jewish communities whose members had been accepted more than a generation ago as French citizens. In 1870, at the behest of the by now unified French Jewish community, the Third Republic conferred full French citizenship on the indigenous Jews of Algeria too, but not on their Arab and Berber neighbors.

Nineteenth-century overseas empire building and consolidation—by the regimes with wide (male) suffrage—started with this fixed identity barrier so difficult to breach. Even as they grew more liberal Britain, the United States, and France practiced a politics of difference. Add to that the emergence around midcentury of "scientific" racial barriers—in France, biology was the science most republicans held dearest—and we see that difference was imposed on the colonials (and in the United States on domestic African slaves), not chosen by them.

When we are disturbed to hear advocates of Black Nationalism in the United States, or of Caribbean identity in Great Britain, or of the right to difference in France, we should keep in mind that—however undesired by democratic inclusionists today (among whom I count myself)—the minorities from the southern hemisphere did not opt out of identity choices offered them. They were first designated as undesirable for full citizenship by the chiefs of the so-called mother country. Movements of extreme separatisms are expressions of hurt reaction to exclusion. In many cases the excluded take on the imposed identity but change the valence to make "Black beautiful" or an integrist Islam the only valid version of the true faith. So when conservatives speak of the injustice of advantaging minority candidates for education or jobs in the United States or France, or rally to save an endangered laity in France, we should not forget equal opportunity was proclaimed in the Declaration of Independence and the laic republic violated its own principles by labeling Algerians as Muslims when they did not do the same for Protestants, Jews, Sikhs, or Hindus.[7]

So the sahib style was brought back from the colonies to discipline metropolitan societies. The progressive social science of the Enlightenment with its ideal of the noble savage was instrumentalized in the nineteenth- and twentieth-century empires and turned against both provincials in Europe and the ignoble "savages" overseas. As a kind of perverse recompense, the mythology of the third world as a place of peace and safety from increasingly internationalized industrial capitalism—as in Jean Renoir's *The River*—became thematized and made beautiful. Aesthetic modernism lived with colonialism and died with postcolonialism. Although doubtless a great cornucopia of creation, for the first time in Western history, a new arts ideology—modernism— became the alibi for the artist to detach him- or herself from society to become the mysterious woman or the uncommitted flâneur. Like the arsenic great ladies swallowed in the Victorian age to increase their beautiful pallor, aesthetic modernism proved dangerous to the living. In my final essay on cultural history as a project of freedom both at home and overseas, I have tried to show something of what was at stake in the various analyses I offered.

If the praxis of empire benefits rulers but injures democracy, can we think the contrary, that the practice of greater democracy might defeat empire? As I said at the outset, my own answer remains firmly, yes—I hope so. Consider the *humane* capital ready for investment in our account: democratic peoples learning to respect the rights of their fellows and—in our global age—their potential fellows in other parts of the world. Certainly, there are lots of other reasons democracies die: they are conquered, oligarchies seize power, the civic spirit of the population atrophies as cynicism spreads and people seek safety in hermetic private lives. But conquering an empire has historically proven the surest way to corrupt a nation. Athens, Rome, Spain, Portugal, imperial Japan, fascist Italy, Nazi Germany, the Soviet Union, and, I fear, the United States serve as just some examples. The inevitable inequalities of empire destroy the integrative spirit on which democracies are founded.

Currently, Britain and France are trying to integrate what is valuable from the colonial heritage—new citizens, new music, new art, and new foods. And they are trying to master—as the Germans put it—the negative heritage of past colonial engagements. I have dwelt on the return effects to Europe of the colonial situation because today the colonial heritage can cause the most harm to our creating a just and fair society; I see that Orwell's insight, that colonialism is not good for us, is validated by history. But I am well aware—and I hope fully appreciative of—the vast development aid the southern hemisphere has given the north. That boost to European development has to be recompensed.

Decolonization after World War II spread its effects in Europe and America in great expanding circles such as those made by a stone tossed in the water. Procuring needed resources once pursued in the frame of colonialism, slowly turned into patterns of international trade. The making of the U.S. dollar the world's reserve currency after the war at Bretton Woods stabilized world economic transactions for a time. Yet with the creation of hundreds of new nations, the world political system became infinitely more complicated. The great power rivalry had the positive effect at least, of creating a frame for international political discussion. There could not have been a third world if, in vying for power, the United States and Russia had not made of the deadlock a temporarily free space. With the domino-like fall of formal empires in the postwar decades we experienced the parallel and, I think, connected death of European modernism in the arts. Both trends had exhausted their logics and their repertoires. Experimental after-modernisms, after-colonialism, and even an emerging after-primitivism now seem the order of the day.[8]

In conclusion, consider the following morality tale. Beginning in the summer and into the fall of 2003, the part-time culture workers of France went on strike. Bit players, stage technicians, media part-timers, and the like benefit from a special law that gives them the right to collect unemployment insurance even if they have not worked very long before. Occasional work, after all, is the nature of the performing arts. The Raffarin government wanted to suppress these more generous unemployment provisions and subject the *intermittents*, as they are called, to the same rules governing other unemployed members of the population. Seemingly an equitable move, the change would have made the lives of arts workers even more precarious than they already were, thus inevitably cutting back the pool of arts talent to impoverish the quality of the French public arts. Moreover, the change would have done away with the de facto indirect state subsidy to the arts because many *intermittents* continue to work with their theater troupes after they have been formally laid off. The company could benefit from their work, while the *intermittents* lived on their unemployment.

Abuses certainly occurred. Letting people work for, say, three months and then collect unemployment for eight more seems to overcherish arts workers who have not yet entirely proved themselves. Some *intermittents*, living off their liberal unemployment benefits, could afford unconscionable overseas vacation trips. But still we are not talking here about huge pilferage of the people's money. I would hazard a guess that the total level of corruption was far less than a competent tax accountant could hide for a big French corporation; or, one inferior to the perfectly legal state subsidy some of these corporations—in agrobusiness, for example—receive.

Sometimes the *intermittents* struck a festival and closed it down. This happened in the summer of 2003 with the festivals of Avignon, Aix, and Paris Été. Sometimes they blocked individual performances only. Other times, they were content to bring their cause before the public and then let the show go on. This last was the case with a performance on 19 July 2003 of Jean Racine's *Esther* at the Comédie française. It seems that that night a deal had been struck: if a representative of the *intermittents* could speak to the audience before the performance began, they would let the play go on. With the audience settling in for the evening's offering, a group of nine or ten strikers came on stage. A young woman began reading a page-long statement about the why and wherefore of their cause, the injustice of changing their unemployment rights, and about their determination to hang in until they won. Then coming to the end of the document, the speaker exhorted the audience to fight against globalization.

Only in France can I imagine this level of politicization in the arts and this evidence of a sense of how different struggles were connected.

Like the surrealist who early fought against imperialism, young French artists, vulnerable to the market, are prepared to join the fight against neoliberal globalization. The alliance of bit players at the national theater and José Bové and other fighters for an alternative globalization (*alter-mondialistes*), supported by the Greens, the Socialists, and the Communist Party—the marvelous new alliances in a globalized world. All these Europeans are making common cause with the major losers of neoliberal globalization, the economically poor nations of Asia, Africa, and Latin America. Profit-driven American commercial culture has also targeted their cultural fields; it has France's. That alliance seems to me a marvelous way of starting to master the culture of a colonial past—for both the once-colonizers and the once-colonized, and of warding off new kinds of cultural subjugation.

PREFACE

1   At this late date, Niall Ferguson, *Empire: The Rise and Demise of the British World Order and the Lessons for Global Power* (New York: Basic, 2003), reaches back for the old trope of how much the British Empire benefited the colonized, gifting them with, among other important things, the English language. Astonishingly, in Ferguson's tale the colonized played no decisive role in ending empire. Change the country's and colonies' names, and the book can be read as an apologia for the French Empire. Of course, unlike Ferguson's conclusion, the French story would not have ended with an appeal to the United States to follow Rudyard Kipling's advice to us to "pick up the . . . burden." Now based in the United States, this descendent of the Scots who built the British Empire continues to think imperially on our behalf.

2   Chalmers Johnson, *Blowback: The Costs and Consequences of American Empire* (New York: Holt, 2000), 8.

3   Chalmers Johnson, *The Sorrows of Empire: Militarism, Secrecy, and the End of the Republic* (New York: Holt, 2004), 286. More recently, Olivier Le Cour Grandmaison, *Coloniser, Exterminer: Sur la guerre et l'État colonial* (Paris: Fayard, 2005), has demonstrated how the techniques of official terrorism, biological racism, and even a genocidal mind-set, worked out by the generals who pacified Algeria after the conquest, were brought back to metropolitan France to guide, first, the repression of the workers' uprising of 1848, then the Third Republic's repressive policies in the other colonies, and (perhaps not) finally, the racial politics of Vichy France.

4   The reader will find some of my thoughts on these problems, especially immigrant workers and empire, in my *Bringing the Empire Back Home: France in the Global Age* (Durham, NC: Duke University Press,

2004). *Sorrows of Empire* names as harmful consequences of empire in the American case, as well: emphasis on war and terrorism sown and reaped, legitimation crisis of government because it lies to us, and economic disaster (283–312).

5   Peter Padfield, *Maritime Power and the Struggle for Freedom: Naval Campaigns That Shaped the Modern World, 1788–1857* (London: John Murray, 2003). Eric Hobsbawm, "Où va l'Empire américain," *Le Monde Diplomatique*, June 2003, 1, 20–21.

6   Should you, the reader, be tempted either to stop here because these claims may sound familiar, or to continue because they seem comforting, let me just say that you will find no known version of classical Marxism in what follows.

7   See my *Bringing the Empire Back Home: France in the Global Age* (Durham, NC: Duke University Press, 2004), chap. 2.

8   Grammatically, it should, of course, be "Greatest France." But I have taken the liberty of rendering it "Greater France" because the model of the new concept was Britain's—Austin Chamberlain's dream of empire as a Greater Britain. And so I have flouted French grammar to draw attention to the scandal that the way we have written national histories in the past in isolation from parallel happenings in other lands, especially that of the major imperial states, today just makes bad history.

9   This was literally so. Recall his long residence, employment, and association with Anthony Ashley Cooper, Earl of Shaftesbury. Locke had studied medicine and had first won the admiration of Ashley, and an invitation to reside in the household, on account of his medical skills. He went on to become the earl's policy wonk.

10   The statement is widely quoted, as are parts or the whole of the Putney Debates. I took this citation from Samuel Bowles and Herbert Gintis, eds., *Democracy and Capitalism* (London: Routledge Keegan Paul, 1986), 86.

1   SHRINKING COLONIAL ADMINISTRATORS

1   Raymond Gauthereau, *Journal d'un colonialiste* (Paris: Seuil, 1986), 165–67, 178–83. All translations from the French are mine.

2   George Orwell, "Shooting an Elephant," in *Collected Essays*, 2d ed. (London: Seeker and Warburg, 1961), 15–23.

3   See Bernard Crick's several discussions of the degree of historicity, that is, factual truth, in Orwell's stories in his introduction to *Nineteen*

Eighty-Four (Oxford: Clarendon, 1984), 107, where he concludes, I think, rightly, "and does it matter?" For a similar refusal to take too seriously the concern of sorting out fact from fiction in regard to whether a story works or not, also see David Lodge, *Modes of Modern Writing* (London: Edward Arnold, 1977), 9–17.

4   I was a little uncertain about Orwell's story of a *male* elephant in heat. But a kind reply to my inquiry by Marie Monaghan of the Library of the Zoological Society of London assured me that must, or musth, occurs in male elephants: "[It] is connected to the annual reproductive cycle shown by most elephants which corresponds to the seasonal availability of food following the rains." It is a period of high male hormone levels and aggressive behavior. Must can apparently last two to three months. For the needs of his story, Orwell may have taken liberties with the duration of the passion of his male elephant.

5   David Cannadine, *Ornamentalism: How the British Saw Their Empire* (New York: Oxford University Press, 2001).

6   My claim about the persistence of the ancien régime in the colonial empire needs, I know, fleshing out and documentation. That must be for another time, a future project.

7   Robert Delavignette, *Service Africain*, 4th ed. (Paris: Gallimard, 1946), 127. The first edition was published in 1939 with the title *Le vrais chefs d'un empire*. See also his memoirs, *Soudan, Paris, Bourgogne* (Paris: Grasset, 1935), 133. For a good treatment of this vision of a peasant empire with various local civilizations and its political-colonial effects see, Véronique Dimier, "For a Republic: 'Diverse and Indivisible?' France's Experience from the Colonial Past," *Contemporary European History* 13 (2004): 46–66.

8   Erik H. Erikson's notion of "negative identity," established in his *Young Man Luther: A Study in Psychoanalysis and History* (New York: Norton, 1958), proves useful here. And although Ashis Nandy is speaking of Rudyard Kipling's tortured relation to India, his interpretation applies to many colonial situations, and specifically to Gauthereau's: "Colonialism tried to take over the consciousness, to make it congruent with the needs of colonialism, to take away the wholeness of every white man who chose to be a part of the colonial machine, and to give him a new self-definition which, while provincial in its cultural orientation, was universal in its geographical scope. In retrospect, colonialism did have its triumph after all. It did make Western man definitively non-Eastern and handed him a self-image and a world view. . . . He could not but be non-Eastern . . . his negative identity." Ashis Nandy, *The Intimate Enemy: Loss and Recovery of Self under Colonialism* (Delhi: Oxford University Press, 1983), 71.

9 Of course, this needs nuancing. In Morocco, for example, at least under the influence of its great governor-general Louis-Hubert Lyautey and his admirers, the French administration tried to freeze the indigenous cultures against too much assimilation, and against too much dangerous self-generated change. See the very interesting thesis on French cultural and educational policy by Spencer Segalla, "Teaching Colonialism, Learning Nationalism: French Education and Ethnology in Morocco: 1912–1956" (PhD diss., State University of New York at Stony Brook, 2003). His several years as a teacher in Morocco have allowed him to understand in profound ways the historic French education project and the Moroccan uses and resistances to it.

10 Not only was there a Lyautey to match Lord Lugard (Frederick Lugard), both advocates of indirect rule but the policies and self-presentation of each state's colonial administration also changed at different conjunctions from the nineteenth century to decolonization. Still, I will stick by my snapshot of the manifest difference of styles when each administrator does the same thing and then tells us about it in his way—in this comparison, the British in Burma in the 1920s and the French in the Ivory Coast in the 1940s. Hopefully, in her completed Oxford dissertation, which compares British and French colonial administrations over time, Véronique Dimier will sharpen our ideas of this, it turns out, very complicated subject. For now, see her "Direct or Indirect Rule: Propaganda around a Scientific Controversy," in *Promoting the Colonial Idea: Propaganda and Visions of Empire in France*, ed. Tony Chafer and Amanda Sackur (London: Palgrave, 2001), 168–83. Here, Dimier backs away from trying to resolve the debates about styles of administration to ask, instead, who, at different moments, made the comparisons, why did they do so, and what was at stake?

11 Crick has more recently found newer and better evidence that supports, at least in part, the claim for the tale's factual origins. See Bernard R. Crick, "Afterthoughts and After Matter," in *George Orwell: A Life* (London: Penguin, 1992), 586–89.

12 See Anna Pondopoulo, "Les représentations françaises sur les Peules et les Haalpulaar'en ('Toucouleurs') du xviiie au début du xxe siècle: Des stéréotypes à la conaissance scientifique" (PhD diss., Université de Paris 7 [Denis Diderot], 2004), 58–59.

13 On the emphasis on character or what she calls esprit de corps in French colonial administration, see Dimier, in *Direct and Indirect Rule*, 173–74.

14 Pierre Messmer, "Note sur la situation morale du Corps des Administrateurs," 14 December 1949, Papiers Delavignette, 19PA, box 3, file 31, Archives Nationales de la France d'Outre-Mer, Aix-en-Provence (hereafter cited as ANFOM). Messmer's usage of the word *morale* is ambiguous. The best reading Mihaela Bacou (of Reid Hall, Paris) and I could make was that Messmer wanted to underline how a serious *morale* problem among colonial administrators had reached the degree of intensity to pose for him and for France serious *moral* questions. Nearly fifty years later, in his memoirs, he had come around to the acceptance of the loss of empire. There is little in this much later text about his attempts to keep the colonies French. Pierre Messmer, *Les blancs s'en vont: Récits de décolonisation* (Paris: Albin Michel, 1998), 9–33.

15 Messmer, ANFOM.

16 Ibid. On the post–World War II crisis in the colonial administration see further J. I. Lewis, "The French Colonial Service and the Issues of Reform," *Contemporary History* 4 (1995): 153–88; Marc Michel, "L'Empire colonial dans les débats parlementaires," in Serge Berstein and Pierre Milza, *L'Année 1947* (Paris: Presses de Science Po, 2000), 187–217.

17 "Le métier d'administrateur des colonies," commissioned by Jacques Christol, annotated by Robert Delavignette, 19 pages, Papiers Delavignette, 19PA, box 16, file 216, ANFOM.

18 On such wholesale psychological exercises in native education in both French East Africa and Morocco, see, most recently, Segalla, "Teaching Colonialism, Learning Nationalism."

19 In English, the *ich* of Freud is normally translated as "the ego"; in French, it becomes the *moi*. The text appears so insightful about how character develops that one could think the author might have gotten this psychology of the subject/Subject from Louis Althusser, who himself lived a devote Catholic childhood and then, without removing this substrate, passed under the influence of Lacanian Freudianism (and Stalinist Marxism). But Althusser's essay on State Ideological Apparatuses, where he develops this theme, was published only some three decades after this report was written, so such a conjecture of intellectual history is a chronological impossibility. Louis Althusser, *Lenin and Philosophy, and Other Essays*, ed. and trans. Ben Brewster (London: New Left Book, 1971), 127–86.

2 BOURDIEU'S CULTURAL REVOLUTION

1 As opposed to, for example, earlier, eighteenth-century, and later, post–World War II, interest in social structures or kinship.

2   On the splitting off of French folk art from other ethnographic displays see the account of Martine Segalen, *Vie d'un muse, 1937–2005* (Paris: Stock, 2005), 7–50. She worked at the research center of the folklore museum from 1967 to 1996, becoming its head from 1986 to 1996.

3   Marcel Fournier, *Marcel Mauss* (Paris: Fayard, 1994), 536–37.

4   See recently on inventing tribes for the sake of colonial rule the doctoral thesis on the Peules of Senegal by Anna Pondopoulo, "Les représentations françaises sur les Peules et les Haalpuaar'en ('Toucoleurs') du xviiie au début du xxe siècle: Des stéréotypes à la connaissance scientifique" (PhD diss., Université de Paris 7 [Jussieu], 2004).

5   From its start to 1936 the largest part of the institute's funding came from the separate budgets devoted to each of the colonies. From 1937 onward, after the loss of the Rockefeller subvention, governmental support came from the metropolitan budget of the Ministry of Colonies. Fournier, *Marcel Mauss*, 694, quoting Lucien Lévy-Bruhl, "Rapport sur l'Institut d'Ethnologie, année scolaire 1936–1937," *Annales de l'Université de Paris*, January–February, 1939, 53.

6   Letter of Sapir to Mauss dated 17 June 1935, quoted in Fournier, *Marcel Mauss*, 632.

7   Michèle Cointet, *L'histoire culturelle de la France, 1918–1958* (Paris: Sedes, 1958), 107.

8   Segalen, *Vie d'un muse*, 51–80.

9   Nina Gorgus, *Le magicien des vitrines: Le muséologie Georges Henri Rivière*, trans. Marie-Anne Codadou (Paris: Maison des Sciences de l'Homme, 2003).

10   Christian Faure, *Le projet culturel de Vichy: Folklore et révolution nationale, 1940–44* (Lyons: Presses Universitaires de Lyon, 1989). Faure had trouble getting this, his thesis, published and finding a university post after its appearance. Finally, he left the academy for publishing.

11   Eric Jennings, *Vichy in the Tropics: Pétain's National Revolution in Madagascar, Guadeloupe, and Indochina* (Stanford, CA: Stanford University Press, 2001).

12   And hence after the war, I would argue, the triumph of the Nouvelle Vague, with its strong American influences.

13   Following in the path of Georges Balandier, see the splendid doctoral thesis of Emmanuelle Saada, "La 'question des métis' dans les colonies françaises : Socio-histoire d'une catégorie juridique (Indochine et autres territoires de l'empire français, années 1890–1950)" (PhD diss., École des Hautes Études en Sciences Sociales, 2001), to be published in Paris by Éditions La Découverte.

14   Wallerstein now sees the value of cultural theory: *The End of the World as We Know It: Social Science for the Twenty-first Century* (Minneapolis: University of Minnesota Press, 1999).

15   This is a reference to the argument of Lucien Lévy-Bruhl (1857–1939) that primitive peoples think fundamentally differently from Westerners. For example, they do not hold what we call the law of identity, that a thing cannot be *A* and non-*A* at the same time. Rather, their magical thinking allows members of such societies to believe marvelous and irrational things. A good blow against the then dominant theory of social evolutionism, and very influential in the 1930s, unfortunately it radically and fundamentally divided humankind into rational and irrational. "De la règle aux strategies: Entretien de Pierre Lamaison avec Pierre Bourdieu," *Terrain*, no. 4 (1985): 93–100.

16   Pierre Bourdieu, brief comment in the course of the conference, *Le mal de voir: Ethnologie et orientalisme, politique et épistémologie, critique et autocritique; Contributions aux colloques orientalisme, africanisme, américanisme, 9–11 mai 1974, ethnologie et politique au Maghreb, 5 juin 1975* (Paris: Union Générale d'Éditions, 1976), 92.

17   Pierre Bourdieu, *Esquisse pour une auto-analyse* (Paris: Raison d'Agir, 2004), esp. 53–108.

18   I owe this anecdote to Gisèle Sapiro, who herself did her thesis with Bourdieu and heard him tell the story.

19   Pierre Bourdieu, "Les conditions sociales de la production sociologique: Sociologie coloniale et décolonisation de la sociologie," concluding remarks, *Le mal de voir*, 422.

20   See, for example, Pierre Bourdieu et al., *The Weight of the World: Social Suffering in Contemporary Society*, trans. Priscilla Pankhurst Ferguson (Oxford: Polity, 1999).

21   Pierre Bourdieu, "L'identité et la représentation : Eléments pour une réflexion critique sur l'idée de région," *Actes de la Recherche en Sciences Sociales*, no. 35 (1980): 63–72.

22   On the crisis of postcoloniality in the social sciences, both in theory and in jobs, see further Herman Lebovics, *Bringing the Empire Back Home: France in the Global Age* (Durham, NC: Duke University Press, 2004), chaps. 2, 3.

3   RENOIR'S VOYAGE OF DISCOVERY

1   Stephen Greenblatt, "Towards a Poetics of Culture," in *The New Historicism*, ed. H. Aram Vesser (New York: Routledge, 1989), 12.

2   The phrase is Henry Rousso's, *Le syndrome de Vichy de 1944 à nos jours* (Paris: Seuil, 1987), 42–48; translated byArthur Goldhammer as *The Vichy Syndrome: History and Memory in France since 1944* (Cambridge, MA: Harvard University Press, 1991).

3   I first heard the word used as a student to describe individuals, like myself, who, with all sorts of motives, moved between East and West Berlin in the days of the cold war. They mocked the boundaries to their benefit. Carrying a U.S. passport, I got to leave the stuffy and culture-dead Germany of the Economic Miracle (*Wirtschaftswunder*) to see Brecht plays at the Berliner Ensemble and repertory companies doing German classical theater and music. Other *Grenzgänger* traded on the black market or spied. But neither Germany wanted to expose its citizens to what was valuable on the other side of the armed border.

4   I draw here on the work of Jonathan Buchsbaum, "'My Nationality Is Cinematography': Renoir and the National Question," *Persistence of Vision*, nos. 12–13 (1996): 29–48.

5   Peter Bürger and Christa Bürger, *The Institutions of Art*, trans. Loren Kruger (Lincoln: University of Nebraska Press, 1992). The Bürgers' sense of the institution of art resembles Dudley Andrew's characterization of Renoir as an institution.

6   Dudley Andrew, *Mists of Regret: Culture and Sensibility in Classic French Film* (Princeton, NJ: Princeton University Press, 1995), 274.

7   Quoted in Julian Jackson, *The Popular Front in France* (Cambridge: Cambridge University Press, 1988), 66.

8   Maurice Thorez, *France of the People's Front and Its Mission in the World* (New York: Workers Library, 1938), 9–10.

9   Marcel Pagnol, who owned a large production facility just outside of Marseilles, made studio space, equipment and technicians available to Renoir.

10   Alexander Sesonske, *Jean Renoir: The French Films, 1924–1939* (Cambridge, MA: Harvard University Press, 1980), 165–84. Andrew, *Mists of Regret*, 206, following André Bazin, credits *Toni* with influencing the flowering of Italian neorealist films after World War II. Bazin's argument is in his "Une esthétique de la réalité" in his *Qu'est-ce que le cinéma?* (Paris: Cerf, 1957), 128. The film was based on an actual *fait divers* that an old friend of Renoir's, the Martigues chief of police who was also a writer (only in France!), had told him about.

11   Buchsbaum, "'My Nationality Is Cinematography.'" Andrew, *Mists of Regret*, 207–9.

12   Quoted in Sesonske, *Jean Renoir*, 325. After *Toni,* Renoir made his

Le Crime de Mr. Lange (1935). It is a beautiful film and has the famous 360 degree camera shot, which is still wonderful to see. But the film's anarcho-cooperative theme—that the workers can run the print shop as a cooperative better than the malicious owner—is one that Renoir quickly left behind as he grew closer to the Communist Party the following year. I thank Phil Nord for encouraging me to comment on this film, which represents a different political sense than the apolitical humanism of *Toni* and the Popular Front films Renoir made when he was closest to the PCF.

13 Jean Kress interview of Jean Renoir, "Une heure avec un maître du cinema français: Jean Gabin," *L'Avant-Garde*, 13 March 1937, 1, 5; the quotation 5.

14 Jean Renoir, *My Life and My Films*, trans. Norman Denny (New York: Atheneum, 1974), 127. The English text translates *générosité* as "warmheartedness"; I think in this context the word *goodwill* better conveys the sense of this special French idea.

15 Georges Lefèbvre's early treatment of the revolution was published in a widely diffused and highly influential series called "Peuples et Civilisations" ("Peoples and Civilizations"). His *La révolution française* (Paris: Alcan, 1930) was published in books 1 and 2 of volume 13. In 1932 he published *La grande peur de 1789* (Paris: Colin, 1932), the first volume of his great synthetic work. In the same year Renoir was filming *La Marseillaise* (released in 1938), Lefèbvre put out another volume, *Les Thermidoriens* (Paris: Colin, 1937). He also wrote a volume for the 150th anniversary of the French Revolution, *Quatre-vingt-neuf* (Paris: Maison du Livre Français, 1939).

16 Thorez, *France of the People's Front*, 55–56.

17 François Furet, *Penser la révolution française* (Paris: Gallimard, 1978).

18 See the polemic about the polemics of the period by Steven Laurence Kaplan, *Farewell, Revolution: The Historians' Feud; France, 1789/1989* (Ithaca, NY: Cornell University Press, 1995). Daniel Bell, *The End of Ideology: On the Exhaustion of Political Ideas in the Fifties* (New York: Free Press, 1960).

19 Thorez, *France of the People's Front*, 32.

20 Quoted in Roger Shattuck's essay, "Having Congress: The Shame of the Thirties," in *The Innocent Eye: On Modern Literature and the Arts* (New York: Farrar, Straus Giroux, 1984), 4.

21 Ibid., 6.

22 Julian Jackson, *The Popular Front in France* (Cambridge: Cambridge University Press, 1988), 70.

23 Pascal Ory, "La politique culturelle du Front Populaire français (1935–1938)" (PhD diss., Université de Paris 10 (Nanterre), 1990), 1654. This was published in shortened form as *La belle illusion: Culture et politique sous le signe du Front Populaire, 1935–1938* (Paris: Plon, 1994), but all my citations are to the more complete dissertation version.

24 Of course, any French person, or historically knowledgeable foreigner, seeing the film could name incidents and other personalities represented or implied in the scenario. Nevertheless, having just arrived, tired, perhaps a bit overwhelmed by Paris, for Arnaud, the volunteers' political voice, to name Robespierre as the public figure about whose activities the southern revolutionaries wish to know makes this the most important statement of the film on the politics of the Revolution. If such a film were made today, I suspect someone in it would ask about the Marquis de Sade, an activist in his Paris section, and/or the ultraleftist Gracchus Babeuf, and/or Olympe de Gouges, who, in 1793, the year after the moment portrayed in *La Marseillaise*, the Jacobins guillotined for her unseemly feminism. And such a parallel personification of political values would show that filmmaker and perhaps some of his or her audience were interested in a different revolution than Renoir's or that of the French labor confederation. Joan Landes has argued, for example, that the (male) Jacobins pushed women out of the public sphere, where in the eighteenth century they had played a significant role. Joan Landes, *Women and the Public Sphere in the Age of the French Revolution* (Ithaca, NY: Cornell University Press, 1988). Although she accepts some of Landes's judgments about the Revolution's harm to women, Lynn Hunt has more recently argued that in the longer term, by creating a legal and moral context of human rights, the French Revolution helped emancipate women. See the concluding section of her *The Family Romance of the French Revolution* (Berkeley: University of California Press, 1992). And on the radical implications of the writings of de Sade and his fellow pornographers, see her introduction to the conference papers she edited, *The Invention of Pornography: Obscenity and the Origins of Modernity, 1500–1800* (New York: Zone Books, 1993), 9–48. Hunt has also published a documentary history on the growth of ideas and practices of human rights in the revolutionary era, *The French Revolution and Human Rights: A Brief Documentary History* (New York: St. Martin's, 1996).

25 The PCF played a leading role in actively promoting the major cultural innovation of the Popular Front, that of greatly and permanently enhancing the state's administrative and financial responsibility for cultural life. See Ory, "La politique culturelle," 1636–39.

26   These debates are presented in part in Ernst Bloch et al., *Aesthetics and Politics* (London: NLB, 1977).

27   Jonathan Buchsbaum, *Cinema Engagé: Film in the Popular Front* (Urbana: University of Illinois Press, 1988), 233.

28   Quoted in Sesonske, *Jean Renoir*, 325.

29   The German Communist Party had not closed itself off in this way. Writing during the Popular Front, Brecht, in particular, strongly condemned the political betrayal that went with the Left's accepting the culture of the bourgeoisie. "Wer in unserer Zeit *statt Volk Bevölkerung und statt Boden Landbesitz* sagt, unterstützt schon viele Lügen nicht. Er nimmt den Wörtern ihre faule Mystik" (Those in our time who say *population instead of Volk and property instead of the land*) already provide no support for many lies. They remove their lazy mysticism from these words). The passage comes from Brecht's *Fünf Schwierigkeiten beim Schreiben der Wahrheit* (1938), and I quote it from Albrecht Betz, *Exil und Engagement: Deutsche Schriftsteller im Frankreich der dreissiger Jahre* (Munich: Edition Text und Kritik, 1986), 11.

30   For communists, the ex-surrealist André Thirion pointedly noted in his memoirs, "family life, the artwork on French banknotes, movie serials, and modesty were as sacred as the verses of the International." See André Thirion, *Revolutionaries without Revolution*, trans. Joachim Neugroschel (New York: Macmillan, 1975), 113. See further the paper by Denis Milhau, onetime member of the PCF, "Reflets de la crise du reflet," in *L'art face à la crise, 1929–1939*, ed. Louis Roux (Saint-Etienne, France: Centre Interdisciplinaire d'Études et des Recherches sur l'Expression Contemporaine, 1980), 241–93, especially the discussion of Maurice Thorez's thoughts on the mission of the French proletariat to replace the faltering bourgeoisie in defense of the national interest and of "our cultural heritage," 262.

31   Thorez, *France of the People's Front*, 10–11.

32   Since the 1880s, more or less without interruption (except under Vichy), the cultural version of the republican contract, as Gérard Noiriel has written about it, has historically been offered by the republic to ethnic provincials (the Catalans, the Alsatians, the Italian-speakers of Nice) and immigrants. It calls on the new French to give up their old personal identity, or leave it at home, and embrace the *civilisation* of France. Inceasingly today's democrats see that contract, as not easily, nor justly, applicable to new candidates for inclusion in the nation. And so, once again, all debate what is French, what should be French. See Gérard Noiriel, *Le creuset français: Histoire de l'immigration XIXᵉ–XXᵉ siècles* (Paris: Seuil, 1988). See

the excellent study by Patrick Weil, who, from the eighteenth century to the present, addresses the changing legal question of what the French state considers a French person: Patrick Weil, *Qu'est-ce qu'un Français: Histoire de la nationalité française depuis la révolution* (Paris: Grasset, 2002). The puzzle in present-day France is, of course, whether the Arab and African populations will follow the precedent of the other groups and whether those already French will accept them. In 2003, under the presidency of Jacques Chirac, a study commission was enpanelled to address the questions of where the line should be drawn today between the laical republic and religious manifestations. The 2004 report of the Commission de Reflexion sur l'Application du Principe de Laïcité dans la République, chaired by Bernard Stasi (the country's ombudsman) and so generally referred to as the Stasi Commission proposed twenty measures for making Muslims, and members of other religions as well, feel welcome in the secular republic and school system. Punitively, the conservative legislature passed only the prohibition against wearing the veil in public schools. The government refused to allow consideration of any of the suggestions for conciliatory gestures, such as halal meals in the cafeterias and the recognition of any Islamic or Jewish religious days as national holidays. Stasi submitted the report to President Chirac on 11 December 2003 and it was published on 5 February 2004. It may be found on the government's printing office website: www .ladocfrancaise.gouv.fr/brp/notices/034000725.shtml. However, the question is being addressed in a more indirect way, as well. In 2003, President Chirac asked another panel to study the feasibility of a study center and museum of immigration, which is now, in 2006, being created.

33 Clifford Browder, *André Breton: Arbiter of Surrealism* (Geneva: Droz, 1967), 14; Thirion, *Revolutionaries without Revolution*, 252; quotations from 330 and 331 respectively.

34 On the politics of prose style, I have found valuable Elizabeth Vihlen's unpublished 1996 study, "Novel Politics: Louis Aragon, Louis-Ferdinand Céline, and the Style of Literature as Politics in French Modernism." See further, Russell A. Berman, *Modern Culture and Critical Theory: Art, Politics, and the Legacy of the Frankfurt School* (Madison: University of Wisconsin Press, 1989), 105–16.

35 Quoted in Ory, "La politique culturelle," 177. See also 191–219. Jackson, *The Popular Front in France*, 113, 120, 126.

36 Initially asked, Breton, leader of the surrealists, had had his invitation to speak withdrawn because some days before the opening session he had slapped Ehrenburg on the street for slandering both his movement and Breton personally in print. In retaliation, Ehrenburg had threatened to end the participation of the Soviet delegation if Breton were allowed to speak. Breton's friend, Paul Éluard, who would join the PCF the next year and so was becoming acceptable to the party, was permitted to read Breton's address on his friend's behalf. But it was past midnight when finally Éluard was allowed on the podium to read Breton's text. As he began, the lights in the hall suddenly went out. An official-type took the platform to announce that the meeting (that is, Éluard reading Breton) could not continue, as the space had been rented only to midnight. They were closing for the evening. André Breton, "Speech to the Congress of Writers (1935)," in *Manifestoes of Surrealism*, trans. Richard Seaver and Helen R. Lane (Ann Arbor: University of Michigan Press, 1969), 237.

37 See my *True France: The Wars over Cultural Identity, 1900–1945* (Ithaca, NY: Cornell University Press, 1992), chap. 2. Breton had gone to discuss future governmental policies with Léon Blum on the Popular Front's taking office. Instead, the premier, a man of letters himself, brought the conversation around to literature, to the surrealist's frustration.

38 When France fell to the German attack in 1940 and the Vichy government was formed, Pétain literally justified his taking power as a gift of his person to the French people. With the "true" France finally in power—and Maurras celebrated Vichy in precisely that language—the Left only knew to claim that it was even more French and more patriotic than Vichy. In London, Charles de Gaulle, for his part, broadcast that France was, for the moment, there in his BBC studio.

39 See Christopher Faulkner's discussion of how Renoir creates the frame of a classical comedy of manners and then formally disrupts it. Christopher Faulkner, *The Social Cinema of Jean Renoir* (Princeton, NJ: Princeton University Press, 1986), 106–22.

40 *La bête humaine*, made by Renoir in 1938 and based on Émile Zola's dark novel, scarcely provides a positive picture of workers, workers' culture, or the possibilities of social change—despite his protests that journalists misunderstood it. See Faulkner, *The Social Cinema*, 101–3; Raymond Durgnat, *Jean Renoir* (Berkeley: University of California Press, 1974), 172–84; and Andrew, *Mists of Regret*, 298–317.

41 I have based my account of Renoir's not yet totally elucidated last months in France largely on Janet Bergstrom, "Jean Renoir's Return to France," *Poetics Today*, no. 17 (1996): 464–65. Commenting on *The River*, Renoir wrote in *Cahiers du Cinéma*, 8 (January 1952), "Before the war, my own way of participating in this universal concert was to try to add my voice to the protest. I do not think that my criticisms were ever very sharp. I love humanity too much and, I dare hope, that I always managed to mix a bit of

tenderness with my sarcasm. Today, the new being that I am realizes that these are not the times for sarcasm, and that the only thing that I can contribute to this illogical, irresponsible, and cruel universe is my 'love.'" "Renoir, On me demande . . . ," *Cahiers du Cinéma*, no. 8 (January 1952); reprinted (in two parts with different names) in *Écrits, 1926–1971* (Paris: Pierre Belfond, 1974). The quotation is from 62.

42 The other part of his essay/interview was printed in the same volume, as "Le Fleuve," *Écrits, 1926–1971*, Quotations, 62.

43 Christopher Faulkner has obtained some of the FBI records on Renoir during his years in Hollywood. Renoir supported organizations suspect to various communist-hunting legislative committees and frequently socialized with the Left émigré community. He surely still considered himself a man of the Left in the war years and a little after. But Faulkner thinks that *The River* was his capitulation to the Truman Era red scare. Christopher Faulkner, "An Archive of the (Political) Unconscious," *Canadian Journal of Communication* 26, no. 1 (2001): 1–16; accessed online at www.cjc-online.ca.

44 Janet Bergstrom roundly criticizes the social autism, especially the rampant sexism of the film, as a double regression for Renoir, one "both personal and social." For example, Jean Gabin, the lead, gets to betray but keep all his cloying mistresses, while achieving a huge success exhibiting them dancing the provocative cancan on stage. Bergstrom, "Jean Renoir's Return to France," 486.

45 Jean Renoir in *La flèche de Paris*, 30 May 1936, quoted in Claude Gauteur, *Jean Renoir: La double méprise, 1925–1939* (Paris: Les Éditeurs Français Réunis, 1980), 52.

46 Tom Gunning, "Varieties of Renoir," in *Persistence of Vision*, 175.

4 FRANCE'S BLACK VENUS

1 Fredric Jameson has demonstrated this relationship between Anglo-Irish literature and Empire. But just as important sectors of the imperial economy are hidden from view overseas, making a totalizing view of national life and culture impossible to render, he finds determining the etiology of the relationship of aesthetic modernism and empire also structurally elusive. "The traces of imperialism can . . . be detected in Western modernism, and are indeed constitutive of it; but," he argues, "we must not look for them in the obvious places, in content, or representation." See his "Modernism and Imperialism" in Seamus Deane, ed., *Nationalism, Colonialism,*

and Literature (Minneapolis: University of Minnesota Press, 1990), 43–56; quotation on page 64.

2 Jürgen Habermas, "Modernity an Incomplete Project," in *The Anti-Aesthetic: Essays on Postmodern Culture*, ed. Hal Foster (New York: New Press, 2002), 3.

3 In the introduction to his *The Condition of Postmodernity: An Enquiry into the Origins of Cultural Change* (Oxford: Blackwell, 1989), vii–ix, David Harvey distinguishes between modernism (the arts), modernity (society), and modernization (a theory of development). In those cases in which it is important to keep separate base and superstructure, these prove useful distinctions. But here, the social aesthetic and colonial converge. Accordingly, I will use *modernism* and *modernity* as designations for overlapping social phenomena.

4 E. P. Thompson, "Time, Work Discipline, and Industrial Capitalism," in *Customs in Common: Studies in Traditional Popular Culture* (New York: New Press, 1993), 352–403.

5 Michel Foucault takes Baudelaire as both the model interpreter and model writer of modernity. See his "What Is Enlightenment," in *The Foucault Reader*, trans. and ed. Paul Rabinow (New York: Pantheon, 1984), 39–42.

6 Walter Benjamin, "Some Motifs in Baudelaire," in *Illuminations*, trans. Harry Zohn, ed. Hannah Arendt (New York: Schocken, 1968), 162.

7 Robert D. E. Burton, *Baudelaire and the Second Empire: Writing and Revolution* (Oxford: Clarendon, 1991), v–xv, 353–66. Burton follows Baudelaire's politics to the end of his life, at which point he wonders whether the poet had ended as a kind of apolitical fascist of the sort described by Zev Sternhell, in his intellectual history of the French radical Right, *Ni droite ni gauche: l'Idéologie fasciste en France* (Paris: Ed. Complexe, 1987). I think this judgment is just as inappropriate to Baudelaire as Burton's characterizations of his earlier "Leftist" views. Burton finds influences from Pierre Proudhon, Edgar Allan Poe, and later and more enduringly, from Joseph de Maistre. Standard political categories make no sense in the poet's case. Burton has nothing to say about Baudelaire's colonial politics or the politics of his relations with Jeanne Duval. Foucault is not brought in to help either. Burton is following new German scholarship on Baudelaire, above all the work of Dolf Oehler, *Pariser Bilder, 1830–1848: Antibourgeoise Ästhetik bei Baudelaire, Daumier und Heine* (Frankfurt/Main: Suhrkamp, 1979). More on Oehler and others who parallel his reading may be found in the review by Claude Pichois, "Baudelaire devant la socio-critique ouest-allemande," *Études Baudelairiennes* 9 (1981): 226–33. See further Jean-Paul

Sartre's brilliant existentialist-psychological essay on Baudelaire, *Baudelaire*, trans. Martin Turnell (London: Horizon, 1949).

8   Walter Benjamin, "Paris, the Capital of the Nineteenth Century," in *Reflections: Essays, Aphorisms, Autobiographical Writings*, ed. and transl. Peter Demetz (New York: Schocken Books, 1986), 146–86. To the degree I can follow his rhetorical gyres, T. J. Clark's recruitment of Baudelaire for the revolution—if for a debordian sort of transformation—may make us feel a bit better about Baudelaire-in-the-world, even if it does not help us see any political convictions displayed on the poet's shield. It seems to me pointless to look for political meanings in Baudelaire's biography. Rather, he did everything to avoid the political. That is why the empire could be important for him: it was a place free of the divisive politics of metropolitan France, where life was lived deeply and freely. See T. J. Clark, *The Absolute Bourgeois: Artists and Politics in France, 1848–1951* (Greenwich, CT: New York Graphic Society, 1973), 141–77.

9   Eliot meant by this phrase a perfect equivalevence of actions, moment, or symbols in a work of art to a real life emotion. If the author does it right, he argued, the reader or spectator will feel exactly and with full power the emotion(s) generated by the artistic presentation. Thus powerful passions in the real world can be harnessed to energize the poem or play. In the case of Baudelaire, I extrapolate Eliot's notion of this link of life and the art work with—but not only with—the French poet's deep and special feel for the colonial. T. S. Eliot, "Hamlet and his Problems," in his *Sacred Wood: Essays on Poetry and Criticism* (London: Methuen, 1921), 95–103.

10   Brian Friel, *Translations*, 1980, in *Plays One* (London: Faber and Faber, 1996), 418–19; ellipses in the original. I am not in any way claiming that the British remapping of Ireland had anything of modernism in it. But I think it significant that the land that had lost its place names, its autonomy, and its language gave us the great exiled masters of modernism, James Joyce and Samuel Beckett.

11   Habermas, "Modernity an Incomplete Project," 3. In his early writings, Habermas remained remarkably insensitive to the world beyond Europe (or beyond maleness, for that matter). His use of clearly colonial metaphors in the quotation from 1980—was that coming from *his* colonial unconscious?

12   T. Denean Sharpley-Whiting, *Black Venus: Sexualized Savages, Primal Fears, and Primitive Narratives in French* (Durham, NC: Duke University Press, 1999), 63–64.

13   I owe this right-on phrase to Pierre Bourdieu's characterization of Philippe Sollers in a *Libération* article on 27 January 1995. It is reprinted in

Bourdieu's "Soller *tel quel*," in *Acts of Resistance: Against the Tyranny of the Market*, trans. Richard Nice (New York: New Press, 1998), 11–13.

14   Charles Baudelaire, *My Heart Laid Bare and Other Prose Writings*, trans. Norman Cameron, ed. Peter Quennell (London: Weidenfeld and Nicholson, 1950), 57. In *The Eighteenth Brumaire of Louis Napoleon*, Karl Marx puts this period of socioeconomic in-betweenness at the center of his explanation of the mid-century modern dictatorship of Louis Napoleon. Later, Nicos Poulantzas based his theory of fascism on this point in Marx. See Nicos Ar Poulantzas, *Fascism and Dictatorship: The Third International and the Problem of Facism*, trans. Judith White (London: New Left Books, 1974).

15   "Germer mille sonnets dans le coeur des poètes / Que vos grands yeux rendaient plus soumis que vos noirs." From the poem "Une dame Créole," in his *Fleurs du mal*. Unless otherwise noted, all translations are mine. The translations I found too often were done to touch American and English readers, and even to clean up Baudelaire's language, not so much to capture the echoes of French society in the choice of French words. *Black* and *slave* were largely interchangeable words at the time.

16   Enid Starkie, *Baudelaire* (New York: Paragon House, 1958), 67.

17   There is a painting of her by Baudelaire's friend Édouard Manet emphasizing her dark and exotic person. And Baudelaire did a sketch of her from memory in his last year of life, but the two images do not resemble each other greatly.

18   See Gaytri Chakravorty Spivak's subtle reading of his poem "Le cynge" and her deconstruction of some of Baudelaire's texts about Jeanne Duval, in her *A Critique of Postcolonial Reason: Toward a History of the Vanishing Present* (Cambridge, MA: Harvard University Press, 1999), 148–56.

19   René Clevel, "The Negress in the Brothel," trans. Samuel Beckett, in Nancy Cunard, ed., *Negro: Anthology Made by Nancy Cunard, 1931–1933* [reprinted from the original 1934 London edition] (New York: Negro Universities Press, 1969); quotation, 581; reference to Baudelaire, 582.

20   Christopher Miller is useful on Baudelaire's Africanist discourse. See Miller also on the same theme in the poetry of Arthur Rimbaud, who after writing some brilliant early poems, spent the rest of his life as an arms dealer in the colonial Middle East. Christopher Miller, *Blank Darkness: Africanist Discourse in French* (Chicago: University of Chicago Press, 1985).

21   Kimberley J. Healey, *The Modernist Traveler: French Detours, 1900–1930* (Lincoln: University of Nebraska Press, 2003).

22   Caution, one art movement can hide another. This is not an essay about the role of orientalism in French aesthetic history. To be sure, both

movements come out of the colonial experience, but orientalism in the arts is mostly about content and atmosphere; modernism is about the making of art. Some modern artists—Matisse, for example—did works on orientalist themes. As a modernist, he was fascinated by the new colors the South let him see. But others, Picasso, for example, took from the colonies to produce new forms without taking the rest of the orientalist pictorialist baggage. On orientalist art, see Roger Benjamin, *Orientalist Aesthetics: Art, Colonialism, and French North Africa* (Berkeley: University of California Press, 2003). I offer the same caveat on the outpouring of colonial films in the interwar years so well treated by David Slavin's *Colonial Cinema and Imperial France, 1919–1939: White Blind Spots, Male Fantasies, and Settler Myths* (Baltimore, MD: Johns Hopkins University Press, 2001). He discusses the racist and antiwoman effect of these films well, as well as giving fine-grained analyses of important films. But, as far as I know, there is no modernist aesthetic news to tell about them.

23   See, for a start, the catalogue of William Rubin's 1986 show, *"Primitivism" in Twentieth Century Art: Affinity of the Tribal and the Modern* (New York: Museum of Modern Art, 1988), which itself constitutes a document of the story of modernism in Europe and colonialism overseas. As corrective, see Mark Antliff and Patricia Leighten, *Cubism and Culture*, rev. ed. (London: Thames and Hudson, 2002).

24   Elizabeth Ezra, *The Colonial Unconscious: Race and Culture in Interwar France* (Ithaca, NY: Cornell University Press, 2000). Ezra argues that French culture had "devoured" the colonial culture, "making it an integral part of itself" (3). And because signs of this absorption were everywhere, she notes, it was "nearly imperceptible" (9). See also 99, 125–26.

25   On the film, see Sharpley-Whiting, *Black Venus*, III–18. Could the baby have been de Mirecourt's, perhaps a subtle way of showing how ethnic mixing is integral to making the French-colonial pair? Elizabeth Ezra kindly e-mailed this answer to my query: "There is no doubt in my own mind . . . that the viewer is meant to get the impression that the baby's father is Tahar, Aouina's North African love interest." I agree with her.

26   It works very much the way, later, Foucault described the simultaneous incitement to sexual activity in the confessional while at the same moment forbidding its expression outside the supervision of the church.

27   See most recently, Petrine Archer-Straw, *Negrophilia: Avant-Garde Paris and Black Culture in the 1920s* (London: Thames and Hudson, 2001); Ean Wood, *The Josephine Baker Story* (London: Sanctuary, 2001); and Tyler Stovall, *Paris Noir: African Americans in the City of Light* (Boston: Houghton Mifflin, 1996).

28 The Surrealist Group in Paris (signed by André Breton, Roger Caillois, René Char, René Crevel, Paul Eluard, J.-M. Monnerot, Benjamin Pèret, Yves Tanguy, André Thirion, Pierre Unik, Pierre Yoyotte), "Murderous Humanitarianism," trans. Samuel Beckett, in Cunard, ed., *Negro*, 575.

29 Understanding the connection of modern Western culture and colonial domination, the surrealists dreamt—earlier than most of the Left—of reversing the relations of power, of liberation from the bourgeoisie with the help of the passion of that selfsame colonial primitive. Although meditating on black women in metropolitan brothels, René Clevel could have been describing his feelings watching Josephine Baker dance as he wrote of the "music of the sea," of "the inexorable vibrations of a distant wave that hastens to engulf every capitalist fortress, from brothel to cathedral." René Clevel, "The Negress in the Brothel," 583.

30 See, for example, my *True France: The Wars over Cultural Identity, 1900–1945* (Ithaca, NY: Cornell University Press, 1992), chap. 2.

31 On fascist modernism in the United States, see the splendid and still valuable book on the Southern "I'll take my stand" writers and critics, Alexander Karanikas, *Tillers of a Myth: Southern Agrarians As Social and Literary Critics* (Madison: University of Wisconsin Press, 1966). More recently, for the reactionary modernism of William Butler Yeats, Ezra Pound, D. H. Lawrence, and T. S. Eliot, see Louise Blakeney Williams, *Modernism and the Ideology of History: Literature, Politics, and the Past* (Cambridge: Cambridge University Press, 2002).

32 Eric Jennings, *Vichy in the Tropics: Pétain's National Revolution in Madagascar, Guadeloupe, and Indochina* (Stanford, CA: Stanford University Press, 2001).

33 See the excellent study by Gisèle Sapiro, *La guerre des écrivains, 1940–1953* (Paris: Fayard, 1999).

34 In this regard, it is useful to recall that Roland Barthes, in the 1960s and 1970s, perhaps the most incisive herald of the death of the author and of the evacuation of meaning in the West, was a scholar of Greek and Roman classics. Was his semiological writing an elegant form of revenge for the work he could no longer do, a bit like that of the minister's son, Friedrich Nietzsche, who elaborated and, finally, celebrated, but also mourned, the death of God?

35 In a *méchant* (mean-spirited) phrase, Edmund Wilson once suggested that postwar French existentialist despair was fueled by the nation's loss of world power status.

36 Jean-François Lyotard, *La condition postmoderne: Rapport sur le sa-*

voir (Paris: Minuit, 1979). The study had been commissioned by the minister of culture of Quebec.

37 Bruno Latour, *We Have Never Been Modern*, trans. Catherine Porter (Cambridge, MA: Harvard University Press, 1993). I prefer my more clunky rendering of Weber's word to "disenchantment," with its strong overtone of the loss of belief. Weber is making a statement about a change in the bases of social organization, not writing intellectual history.

38 Jean-Loup Amselle, *Affirmative Exclusion: Cultural Pluralism and the Rule of Custom in France*, trans. Jane Marie Todd (Ithaca, NY: Cornell University Press, 2003).

39 After receiving little or no cooperation from French authorities, Paxton began going through the files of the German occupier, which provided top quality information. *Vichy France: Old Guard and New Order, 1940–1944* (New York: Knopf, 1972). Robert O. Paxton recently published what is now the best book on the phenomenon of fascism, *The Anatomy of Fascism* (New York: Knopf, 2004).

40 An unfortunate contemporary example: In a legal complaint filed in 1981, deportation survivors charged Maurice Papon with the principle responsibility for organizing the deportation to Nazi death camps of Jews rounded up in the southwest while serving as an official in Vichy Bordeaux. Protectors high in government, including François Mitterrand, hindered his prosecution for crimes against humanity. Finally, in 1998, nearly twenty years after his indictment, Papon came to trial. A number of distinguished historians, including Robert Paxton, came to Bordeaux to testify to the criminal nature of the Vichy regime and its high administrators. But Henry Rousso, head of the Institut d'Histoire du Temps Présent (Institute of Contemporary History) refused to take part and criticized other scholars' testifying in a judicial proceeding driven by other, nonspoken, accusations. Rousso was referring obliquely to the fact that Papon had served as head of the Paris police on the infamous 17 October 1961, when hundreds of Algerian demonstrators for independence were killed and many of their bodies were dumped into the Seine in a premeditated police operation. No one was ever charged in these deaths. He was still in charge of "the forces of order" arrayed against the students and young workers in May 1968. Many saw Papon's career as criminal from start to finish. He was found guilty of the Bordeaux charges and sentenced to ten years of prison. Papon is now well over ninety and ill. A recent proposal to have him pardoned has evoked strong polemics in French public life. In an interview in the morning paper ("Papon n'est pas un détenu ordinaire," *Liberation*, 19 January 2001), Rousso has argued that since the trial had been flawed by "its fundamentally political" but disguised desire for vengeance on the part of the sixties activists, Papon should be released from prison. Later that year, September 2001, he was let out for reasons of poor health. So Papon passes from the ranks of convicted war criminals and loyal clerks of social repression to become a dissertation topic.

41 See the article on the so-called Harki law in question by Leatitia Van Eeck, *Le Monde,* 11 February 2005, and the story of the petition, *Le Monde,* 15 April 2005. As for the media, in the summer of 2000, Radio France Culture did a two-hour remote on French colonialism from the former museum of the colonies that had been erected for the Colonial Exposition of 1931. The moderator, Emmanuel Laurentin, began the program with, "For too long have we not spoken of our former colonial empire."

42 Jacques Marseille, *Empire colonial et capitalisme français: Histoire d'un divorce* (Paris: Albin Michel, 1984).

43 When I spoke to Marseille, he told me that his book had brought him no friends. Third world nationalist intellectuals were annoyed that he had represented the colonies as so much bothersome baggage rather than as key to French economic survival, as they then liked to think. Nor did the more pious French Leninists appreciate Marseille's implicit dismissal of the argument of V. I. Lenin's *Imperialism: The Highest Stage of Capitalism* in this way. Still, Marseille's economic argument forces us to think better.

44 *Pace* French patriots, of course, today New Caledonia is a territory of France, much as Puerto Rico forms an integral part of the United States. But for the chicanery and complexity of this belonging, see my *Bringing the Empire Back Home: France in the Global Age* (Durham, NC: Duke University Press, 2004), chap. 1.

45 See most recently Perry Anderson's two long articles in the *London Review of Books* ("Dégringolade," vol. 26, no. 17; "Union Sucrée," vol. 26, no. 18) in which he variously blames the disappearance of de Gaulle and the writings of academics Pierre Nora and François Furet for the cultural fall of France. Anderson regrets the decline of the French grandeur that encouraged de Gaulle's standing up to the U.S. colossus and to Jean-Paul Sartre refusing a Nobel Prize politically tainted by the cold war. I am proposing that we look at the loss of the colonial empire and the still unmastered consequences of that loss for explanations of France's cultural decline.

46 A history of the many French intellectuals who began their lives and careers in North Africa or the colonies would surely give us a marvelous perspective on the shaping of French culture in the colonies. Imagine who Derrida would have been had Vichy not forced him out of the state school system and into a yeshiva. Without the incitement of pilpul in Talmudic studies, can one imagine deconstruction?

47 Derrida has written of his North African childhood, but I know of no larger reflection by him on the practice of colonialism. There is some self-revelation in *Glas*, trans. Richard Rand and John P. Leavey (Lincoln, Nebraska: University of Nebraska Press, 1990), first published in 1974.

48 Rubin, *"Primitivism."* For a brilliant critique of the show, see James Clifford, "Histories of the Tribal and the Modern," in *Predicament of Culture* (Cambridge, MA: Harvard University Press, 1988).

49 The name is taken from a cold war apologia for the United States directed at the third world: Seymour Martin Lipset, *The First New Nation: The United States in Historical and Comparative Perspective* (New York: Norton, 1979).

50 Jean-Hubert Martin, ed. and curator, *Magiciens de la terre* (Paris: Ed. Centre Georges Pompidou, 1989), 8.

51 The quotations are from two long interviews with Martin by Benjamin Buchloh, published in English as "The Whole Earth Show," *Art in America*, May, 1989, 150–58.

52 Paul Rabinow, *French Modern: Norms and Forms of the Social Environment* (Cambridge, MA: MIT Press, 1989).

53 I find Bourdieu's concept of training people systematically to misrecognize the workings of certain social phenomena extremely useful in the story of French colonialism, for the persistence of racism in nineteenth-century America and for understanding the invisibility in the media of the parts of our population who have not shared these past recent years of prosperity "we have all enjoyed." Pierre Bourdieu and Loïc J. D. Wacquant, *An Invitation to Reflexive Sociology* (Chicago: University of Chicago Press, 1992), 51, 160, 171–72, 250, 194–95.

54 On this change in the aesthetic field, see Pierre Bourdieu, *The Field of Cultural Production* (New York: Columbia University Press, 1993), 192–211.

55 Karl Polanyi, *The Great Transformation: The Political and Economic Origins of Our Times* (Boston: Beacon Press, 1944).

56 The point about modernists celebrating older forms of production, is of course, from Fredric Jameson, *Postmodernism, or, The Cultural Logic of Late Capitalism* (Durham, NC: Duke University Press, 1991), 307; I quote Andrea Fabry from her fine doctoral thesis on the imperial in Hungarian modernism, "'I'm Your Dream': Hungarian Modernism and the Dual Monarchy" (State University of New York at Stony Brook, 2005), chap. 3, p. 3.

57 Roger Benjamin, *Orientalist Aesthetics: Art, Colonialism, and French North Africa, 1880–1930* (Berkeley: University of California Press, 2003), 168–70.

58 See the interview James Clifford gave Robert Borofsky in 2000, reprinted in James Clifford, *On the Edges of Anthropology: Interviews* (Chicago: Prickly Paradigm, 2003), 83, where, in a slightly different context, he speaks of "a progressive narrative of modernity."

59 For more on the museum's muddle, see the last chapter of my *Bringing the Empire Back Home*, especially the discussion of Martin's sense that the Musée du Quai Branly is an important piece of a larger move to French postcolonialism, 148–63.

5 LOCKE, IMPERIALISM, CAPITALISM

1 Peter Laslett, *Locke's Two Treatises of Government: A Critical Edition with Introduction and Notes*, 2d ed. (Cambridge: Cambridge University Press, 1970), 319; cited hereafter as *Two Treatises*. All quotations from the "Second Treatise," the chapter "On Property," will be drawn from this edition. Peter Laslett and John Harrison, *The Library of John Locke* (Oxford: Oxford University Press, 1965); cited hereafter as *Locke's Library*. The standard biography remains Maurice Cranston, *John Locke: A Biography* (New York: Longmans, 1957), 153–54.

2 See the first two volumes of Immanuel Wallerstein's series on the world system, *The Modern World-System*, vol. 1, *Capitalist Agriculture and the Origins of the World-Economy in the Sixteenth Century* (New York: Academic Press, 1974), esp. 346–57; and *The Modern World System*, vol. 2, *Mercantilism and the Consolidation of the European World-Economy, 1600–1750* (New York: Academic Press, 1980). Resting on a world-system analysis but attempting to take the perspective of the "discovered" peoples is Eric R. Wolf, *Europe and the People without History* (Berkeley: University of California Press, 1982), esp. 3–23, 158–94.

3 The reader will think of Michel de Montaigne's "De cannibales," in which, some one hundred years before the Glorious Revolution, the French humanist took a position on the New World completely in contradiction with that Locke would take a century later. Montaigne called land wild if it had been cultivated by humankind; only untouched nature was natural. Just because the native peoples of the New World did not practice commerce or use money, he proposed, did they live in harmony with nature: "They only covet so much as their natural necessities require." When they died, they left what they had to the community. Even when they committed acts of cannibalism, they were more humane than we with our tortures and wars. Not noble savages, but noble peoples, for the Europeans were the savages. Montaigne refused to accept the forming vision of a new world system. And his implicit suggestion that we emulate the "cannibals" was not followed in later history. Locke was the more prescient student of imperialism, unfortunately. But then might we consider Montaigne an astute early alternative globalist? Michel de Montaigne, "De cannibales," *Les Essais: Oeurves completes, ed. Michel Eyquem de Montaigne.* Bibliothèque de la Pléiade (Paris: Gallimard, 1962).

4 See Quentin Skinner's "Meaning and Understanding in the History of Ideas," *History and Theory* 8 (1969): 3–53. For a recent appreciation—but also systematic critique—of Skinner's commitment to "ideas in context" and of his long-time refusal to acknowledge that old ideas proposed today do still have a certain valid rapport with their original formulations, see Keith Thomas, "Politics: Looking for Liberty," *New York Review of Books,* 26 May 2005. The methodological premise of Neal Wood's *The Politics of Locke's Philosophy: A Social Study of "An Essay Concerning Human Understanding"* (Berkeley: University of California Press, 1983), offers good guidance: "Dehistoricizing a philosophic classic depoliticizes and dehumanizes it, separating it from any genuine role in the life and conflict of the age and artificially and mechanically divorcing thought from action" (7). Of equal importance is Neal Wood, *John Locke and Agrarian Capitalism* (Berkeley: University of California Press, 1984), which takes us part of the way by seeing Locke as a theorist of early agrarian capitalism (14). I will freely call Locke a liberal thinker, even if his contemporaries did not. The benefit of being a historian is knowing how a line of thought or action in the past turned out. Rather than remaining stuck in the past, in this essay I want to make use of that privilege.

5 The argument about the connection between Lockean liberalism and imperialism of the first version of this essay, "The Uses of America in John Locke's Second Treatise," *The Journal of the History of Ideas* 47 (October–December 1986): 567–81, has been taken up and developed in the work of several later scholars. For example, James Tully, *An Approach to Political Philosophy: Locke in Context* (Cambridge: Cambridge University Press, 1993), 137–76, contains a chapter reprinted in a volume of essays given first at the Christ Church Oxford conference of 1990 marking the three hundredth anniversary (approximately) of the *Two Treatises,* "Rediscovering America: The *Two Treatises* and Aboriginal Rights," in *Locke's Philosophy: Content and Context,* ed. G. A. J. Rogers (Oxford: Clarendon, 1994), 165–

96. See also the article by Kristin Shrader-Frechette, "Locke and Limits of Land Ownership," the *Journal of the History of Ideas* 54 (1993): 201–19. See, most recently, the thoughtful use of and reference to my contribution to the British History in Perspective Series of St. Martin's Press, W. M. Spellman, *John Locke* (New York: St. Martin's, 1997), 116–21, esp. n. 43.

6 Locke, *Two Treatises*, 294. With the important exceptions of Neal Wood and Richard Ashcraft, most recent reinterpretations of Locke's political philosophy have concentrated on refuting the pathbreaking reading in C. B. Macpherson, *The Political Theory of Possessive Individualism: Hobbes to Locke* (Oxford: Clarendon, 1962), of Locke's chapter 5, "Of Property," and have rather seen Locke as a less modern (therefore, noncapitalist) thinker than does Macpherson.

7 Locke, *Two Treatises*, 295. See further Peter Laslett, introduction to ibid., 100.

8 Locke, *Two Treatises*, 303–4.

9 Ibid.

10 Ibid., 305.

11 Ibid., 306. Johannes Rohbeck, "Property and Labour in the Social Philosophy of John Locke," *History of European Ideas* 5 (1984): 65–77. Karl Olivecrona's attempts to place Locke in a Roman law tradition is, I think, incorrect for a man writing in a land of common law and common law definitions of property. See Karl Olivecrona, "Das Meinige nach der Naturrechtslehre," *Archiv für Rechts- und Sozialphilosophie* 59 (1973): 197–201; Karl Olivecrona, "Locke's Theory of Appropriation," *Philosophical Quarterly* 24 (1974): 220, 226; Karl Olivecrona, "Appropriation in the State of Nature: Locke on the Origin of Property," *Journal of the History of Ideas* 35 (1974): 211, 218, 227; Karl Olivecrona, "The Term 'Property' in Locke's *Two Treatises* of Government," *Archiv für Rechts- und Sozialphilosophie* 61 (1975): 110–14.

12 Locke, *Two Treatises*, 306–8. Both Grotius and Pufendorf grounded the transition from common ownership to private property on common consent because they desired to justify government by consent. See M. Seliger, *The Liberal Politics of John Locke* (New York: Praeger, 1969), 181 and 187–98. Locke carefully avoided using this argument of common consent, however, as Robert Filmer, the target of the attack on the "First Treatise," had hit home in his critique of Grotius with the observation that if private property were secured by the consent of mankind, then the withdrawal of that consent by individuals or groups would dissolve all government and throw mankind back to a state of nature. On this point, see further James Daly, *Sir Robert Filmer and English Political Thought* (Toronto: University of

Toronto Press, 1979), 24, 90, 158–59. Daly finds the argument from appropriation used contemporaneously in the anti-Filmer polemic *Patriarchia non Monarcha* (1681) by Locke's good friend James Tyrrell.

13   Locke, *Two Treatises*, 307. Both James Tully, *A Discourse on Property: John Locke and His Adversaries* (Cambridge: Cambridge University Press, 1980), 139, and Keith Tribe, *Land, Labour, and Economic Discourse* (London: Routledge and K. Paul, 1978), 49–50, reject Macpherson's reading of this passage which understands the servant to have sold his labor to the master. Tully argues, "The turf-cutter, who is Locke's servant, does not and cannot alienate his labor activity"; Tribe seeks to distinguish the servant's labor from that of Locke's horse as evidence that Locke meant to analyze the two efforts differently (50–51). Historically, the Tully-Tribe reading leaves the servant with no reason to agree either to cut or not to cut the turf; he appears merely to make a decision to enter a contract to perform a service or not. It is not clear how or why he decides. It is, however, true that Locke's writing on labor gains ideological force by straddling the ambiguity of labor seen as a commodity and labor as activity. On this point, but situating the argument in a dense historical context, see the excellent article by E. J. Hundert, "The Making of Homo Faber: John Locke between Ideology and History," *Journal of the History of Ideas* 33 (1972): 3–22.

14   Locke, *Two Treatises*, 307.

15   Ibid., 308–9. "But if the [property acquired in an early primitive time he referred to sometimes as "in the beginning"] perished, in his Possession, without their due use; if the Fruits rotted, or if the Venison putrified before he could spend it, he offended against the common Law of Nature."

16   Laslett, introduction, 43; and E. J. Hundert, "Market Society and Meaning in Locke's Political Philosophy," *Journal of the History of Philosophy* 15 (1977): 33–44.

17   Locke, *Two Treatises*, 311–12, 319–20. See also Richard Ashcraft's valuable essay, "The *Two Treatises* and the Exclusion Crisis: The Problem of Lockean Political Theory as Bourgeois Ideology," in *John Locke: Papers Read at a Clark Library Seminar, 10 December, 1977*, J. G. A. Pocock and Ashcraft, ed. (Los Angeles: William Andrew Clark Memorial Library, University of California, 1980), 62–63.

18   There is but one compact for the creation of property; Locke has no need for a two-stage theory of property, one for the first ages of the world and one for life in a commonwealth, as Tully suggests he does. All the important agreements, including that of using money, are made in the state of nature. In this essay, I employ the concept of *consent* to mean the agree-

ment of humankind to use money. For its use in Locke's theory of government, see John Dunn, "Consent in the Political Theory of John Locke," *Historical Journal* 10 (1967): 153–82; and John Dunn, *The Political Thought of John Locke* (Cambridge: Cambridge University Press, 1969), 128–51.

19 In one passage he wrote that "Gold, Silver, and Diamonds [were] things which Fancy or Agreement hath put the Value on, more then real Use, and the necessary Support of Life" (*Two Treatises*, 318), thereby giving evidence of his awareness of the dimension of human arbitrariness and even of caprice in the selection of the medium that is to absolve us of our obligations under natural law. On this illogicality, see Karen Iversen Vaughn, *John Locke: Economist and Social Scientist* (Chicago: University of Chicago Press, 1980), 92–93.

20 Whether we locate the center of gravity of the *Two Treatises* in the succession crisis and the years 1679–80, as Laslett persuasively argues (Laslett, introduction, 65), or connect them to the Glorious Revolution and 1690, the date of their anonymous publication, the question of who was to rule the commonwealth, and by what right, pervades Locke's essays. In this regard I must mark my distance from the work of Tribe, *Land, Labour, and Economic Discourse*. This study, which touches on Locke (46–51), attempts a structuralist reading of the economic theorizing and theorists of the epoch. Thus neither history nor authorship matter: "While this book deals with archaic discursive forms, it cannot be said that it is historical. . . . The use of authors and texts in this book is no more than a bibliographical device, enabling the reader to locate the terms and form of discussion as it proceeds" (159–60). This method leads Tribe to conclude that Hobbes and Locke were involved in a discourse that "turn[ed] obstinately on a patriarchal form of organization that had been the currency of 'civil society' since the time of Plato" (51), and thereby to flatten history to an unchanging and predictable set of problems. A similarly overly abstract and ahistorical approach to the history of ideas, also structuralist in basis, is the more nuanced Tully, *A Discourse on Property*, 153. See the elaborate critique in Wood, *Locke and Agrarian Capitalism*, 72–92.

21 Compare John Locke, *Essay Concerning Human Understanding*, ed. Peter H. Nidditch (Oxford: Oxford University Press, 1979), 618–30. In book 2, chapter 1 (104), Locke wrote: "Whence has [the mind] all the materials of Reason and Knowledge? To this I answer in one word, From Experience: In that, all our Knowledge is founded; and from that it ultimately derives it self." In book 4, chapter 11 (630), he wrote, "The Knowledge of our own Being, we have by intuition. The Existence of GOD Reason clearly makes known to us."

22 Locke, *Two Treatises*, 378.

23 Gregory King, *Natural and Political Observations and Conclusions upon the State and Condition of England, 1696* (London, 1896), republished by Peter Laslett, ed., *The Earliest Classics* (Farnborough, Hants.: Gregg, 1973), sections reproduced in Macpherson, *Political Theory of Possessive Individualism*, appendix, 279. D. C. Coleman, "Labour in the English Economy of the Seventeenth Century," *Economic History Review*, 2d series, vol. 8 (1955): 280–95, esp. 283. H. J. Habbakkuk, "English Landownership, 1680–1740," *Economic History Review*, 1st series, vol. 10 (1940): 4; Robert Brenner, "Agrarian Class Structure and Economic Development in Pre-industrial Europe," *Past and Present*, no. 70 (Feb. 1976): 63. Brenner's article ignited a great debate (seven comments/critiques and Brenner's long rejoinder) that raged in the pages of *Past and Present*, nos. 78, 79, 80, 85, and 97. E. S. De Beer, ed., introduction, *The Correspondence of John Locke*, 8 vols. (London: Clarendon, 1976–1989), 1:xxxii, and n. 1; Wood, *The Politics of Locke's Philosophy*, 19, 26; Wood, *Locke and Agrarian Capitalism*, 30. J. P. Cooper, "The Social Distribution of Land and Men in England, 1436–1700," *Economic History Review*, 2d series, vol. 20 (1967): 419–37. F. M. L. Thompson, "The Social Distribution of Landed Property in England since the Sixteenth Century," *Economic History Review*, 2d series, vol. 19 (1966): 505–17. See also E. L. Jones, "Agriculture and Economic Growth in England, 1660–1750: Agricultural Change," in *Agriculture and Economic Growth in England, 1650–1815*, ed. Jones (London: Methuen, 1967), 152–65. Joyce Oldham Appleby, *Economic Thought and Ideology in Seventeenth Century England* (Princeton, NJ: Princeton University Press, 1978), 153–71.

24 Peter Laslett, "John Locke and His Books," in Laslett and Harrison, *Locke's Library*, 4, 15–18, 22–25, 28–29. See further Cranston, *John Locke*, 463; Wood, *The Politics of Locke's Philosophy*, 31–32. In the part of his library on which we have information, perhaps half his books, he had more titles on medicine, his first profession (some 11.1 percent), on law and politics (10.7 percent), and Greek and Latin classics (10.1 percent). But books of religion and theology, constituting 23.8 percent of the Oxford collection, were the largest single category. See Appleby, *Economic Thought and Ideology*, 220–25; Cranston, *John Locke*, 396; Peter Laslett, "John Locke: The Great Recoinage, and the Origins of the Board of Trade, 1695–1698," in *John Locke: Problems and Perspectives; A Collection of New Essays*, ed. John W. Yolton (London: Cambridge University Press, 1969), 137–64; *John Locke: Collected Works*, ed. John Yolton, 9 vols., 2nd reprinted ed. based on 1724 ed. (London: Routledge, 2001), vol. 9 includes a preface, "A Catalogue

and Character of Most Books of Voyages and Travels," written by Locke for the four-volume anthology of his friend Awnsham Churchill's *Collection of Voyages* (London: Awnsham Churchill, 1704). The preface is a long and careful catalogue-style narrative of important voyages and discoveries. In this text Locke supplied elaborately detailed information about useful natural products and trade items, as well as geographical and navigational information. He offered future explorers advice about precautions to take as they undertook new ventures and proposed as yet unexplored regions for future efforts. The essay lists books on voyages and explorations in Latin, Italian, French, Spanish, and English, with detailed critiques of the quality, credibility, and utility of each. See also in volume 9 of the Routledge edition Locke's, "A History of Navigation from its Original to the the Year 1704."

25　De Beer, *The Correspondence of John Locke*, 1:xxxii and n. 1.

26　Wood, *The Politics of Locke's Philosophy*, 26. At Shaftesbury's suggestion, for example, Locke put £200 into the Bahamas Adventurers just before he took up his post as secretary to the Council of Trade and Plantations. He later sold at a profit. Cranston, *John Locke*, 155–56.

27　Cranston, *John Locke*, 153–54.

28　Ibid., 404–10.

29　Laslett, "John Locke," 137–40. A bureaucratic struggle about minor administrative questions touching on the Virginia plantation put Locke on the side of greater self-rule for the colony. One of Locke's concerns at his new post was the proper relation of the Irish to the English economy. The role of Ireland in Locke's thought is discussed in Cranston, *John Locke*, 408–9; Laslett, "John Locke: Problems and Perspectives," 159–60; Hugh Kearney, "The Political Background to English Mercantilism, 1695–1700," *Economic History Review* 12 (1959). See in the *Correspondence* the letters between Locke and his Irish admirer William Molyneux: volume 4 contains sixteen letters to Molyneux; volume 5, thirty; and volume 6, twenty-four more.

30　Locke, *Two Treatises*, 310–11.

31　Ibid.

32　Ibid., 309.

33　Ibid., 310.

34　Ibid., 317.

35　Ibid., 409. See further Seliger, *The Liberal Politics of John Locke*, 11–18. The European image of the Native Americans is ably dissected in Robert F. Berkhofer Jr., *The White Man's Indian: Images of the American Indian from Columbus to the Present* (New York: Knopf, 1978), esp. part 1 and 75. On the sacred significance the Algonquian attributed to wampum and its transformation into a moneylike trade item, see Ruth M. Underhill, *Red Man's America*, rev. ed. (Chicago: University of Chicago Press, 1975), 67–69. In 1725, the Reverend John Bulkley published a preface to Roger Wolcott's *Poetical Meditations at New London* (New London: T. Green, 1725). In this piece (see esp. xii–xiii), he invoked the authority of Locke to justify the claim that New England colonists might hold land without possessing a title granted by the appropriate Indians. In Bulkley's view, the Indian claims on land admittedly justified by virtue of first occupancy had to yield to the superior claims to the same land conferred by the settlers' labor. See further on Locke and the Indians of America, John Dunn, "The Politics of Locke in England and America in the Eighteenth Century," in Yolton, *John Locke*, esp. 71–72. For the implications of equating America with an earlier primitive stage of Old World life, see Ronald L. Meek, "'In the Beginning All the World Was American,'" in *Social Science and the Ignoble Savage* (Cambridge: Cambridge University Press, 1978), chap. 2. Locke could only stake out the field. He did not engage with the obvious question, for instance, what if—following the example of the European settlers—the Indians began to maximize production and enter the settlers' money economy? Must they still lose their ancestral lands? His liberal theoretical successors in the next century framed the two principal answers. Thomas Malthus argued that the peoples of the colonies could never rise above savagery because of the indolence of the men who did not maximize and the looseness of the women, who made themselves available to their lovers without expecting from them hard work and its consequent economic achievement. The other answer, framed also in the eighteenth century by David Doig, among others, proposed essentially the same argument, except that, rather than the immaturity of the savages, it lay the blame on their degeneracy. For how Malthus and the theorists of degeneration applied precisely this same theory of social unworthiness to Britain's working class savages and their shameless consorts, see newly Jenise DePinto, "Re-imagining the Nation and Empire in Early Victorian Britain: Race, Class, and Gender in Condition of England Question" (PhD diss., State University of New York at Stony Brook, 2005), chap. 1. And for arguments—by Tocqueville, Lamartine, and Renan, to name just three men of influence—remarkably similar to those of Locke and his followers justifying as good for social peace in France the seizure and colonization of Algeria by the French from its first conquest in 1930 onward, see Olivier Le Cour Grandmaison, *Coloniser, Exterminer: Sur la guerre et l'État colonial*

(Paris: Fayard, 2005), 12–17. He quotes Renan, for example—"Une nation qui ne colonise pas est irrévocablement vouée au socialisme" (15)—and discusses Tocqueville's fear of worker radicalism and his hopes for reducing the tensions of the "social question" via Algerian colonization (12–13).

36   On the slight immediate impact of the *Two Treatises*, see Martyn P. Thompson, "The Early Reception of Locke's Two Treatises of Government, 1690–1705," *Political Studies* 24 (1976): 184–91. On Locke's standing among contemporaries, see also the nuanced discussion in Dunn, "The Politics of John Locke in England," 45–46. However, by the eighteenth century, Locke had taken his familiar, and altogether appropriate, place as England's greatest political philosopher. J. G. A. Pocock, *Machiavellian Moment: Florentine Political Thought and the Atlantic Republican Tradition* (Princeton, NJ: Princeton University Press, 1975), 423–24, dismisses Locke's political writings as of little importance to the great movement of civic humanism he argues is the key to the Augustan age. I understand why a New Zealander would not appreciate a thinker who saw the colonies only as dumping grounds for British social problems.

37   For example, Dunn, *The Politics of Locke in England*, 53.

38   John Locke, *Letters Concerning Toleration* (London: Millar and Woodfall, 1905), 178. See this more democratic reading, or one at least sympathetic to Irish nationalist claims, in Paschal Larkin, *The Theory of Property in the Eighteenth Century with Special Reference to England and Locke* (Dublin: Cork University Press, 1930), 64.

39   C. B. Macpherson, "Capitalism and the Changing Concept of Property," in *Feudalism, Capitalism, and Beyond*, ed. Eugene Kamenka and R. S. Neale (Canberra: Australian National University Press, 1975), 112–13.

40   Locke, *Two Treatises*, 314–15. Between 1815 and 1890 alone, perhaps 12 million Britons left for the colonies. H. Wesseling, *Le partage de l'Afrique* (Paris: Gallimard, 2002).

6 AMERICANS AND CULTURAL HISTORY

1   Joan W. Scott, " 'Experience,' " in *Feminists Theorize the Political*, ed. Judith Butler and Scott (New York: Routledge, 1992), 22–40.

2   See Patrick Joyce, "History and Postmodernism," *Past and Present*, no. 133 (1991); and Patrick Joyce, "The End of Social History?" *Social History*, no. 20 (1995).

3 See Laura Lee Downs, *Writing Gender History* (London: Hodder Arnold, 2004).

4 "Post-Colonial Museums: How the French and American Models Differ," *History News Network,* http://hnn.us/articles/6939.html

5 Geoff Eley, "De l'histoire sociale au 'tournant linguistique' dans l'historiographie anglo-américaine des années 1980," *Genèses: Sciences Sociales et Histoire,* no. 7 (1992): 163–93.

6 Eric Hobsbawm, "Perspectives on the Twentieth Century," lecture presented at the monthly Seminar on the International History of the Working Class, Columbia University, 18 November 1992.

7 See, for example, Joan Landes, *Women and the Public Sphere in the Age of the French Revolution* (Ithaca, NY: Cornell University Press, 1988); and Joan W. Scott, *Gender and the Politics of History* (New York: Columbia University Press, 1988).

8 See Robert Darnton, *The Literary Underground of the Old Regime* (Cambridge, MA: Harvard University Press, 1982); Robert Darnton, *The Great Cat Massacre and Other Episodes in French Cultural History* (New York: Basic Books, 1984); Jeremy Popkin, "The Concept of Public Opinion in the Historiography of the French Revolution: A Critique," *Storia della Storiografia* 20 (1991): 77–92; and Craig Calhoun, ed., *Habermas and the Public Sphere* (Cambridge, MA: Harvard University Press, 1993).

9 Michel Foucault, "What is Enlightenment?" in Paul Rabinow, ed., *The Foucault Reader* (New York: Pantheon, 1984), 32–50.

10 Peter Schöttler, conversation with the author.

11 François Cusset, French Theory: *Foucault, Derrida, Deleuze & Cie et les mutations de la vie intellectuelle aux Etats-Unis* (Paris: La Découverte, 2003).

12 See Herman Lebovics, *Bringing the Empire Back Home: France in the Age of Globalization* (Durham, NC: Duke University Press, 2004).

13 See Ranajit Guha, ed., *A Subaltern Studies Reader, 1986–1995* (Minneapolis: University of Minnesota Press, 1997); and Frederick Cooper and Ann Laura Stoler, eds., *Tensions of Empire: Colonial Cultures in a Bourgeois World* (Berkeley: University of California Press, 1997).

14 See chapter 2 of the present volume.

AFTERWORD

1 The best French proponent of this view is Jacques Marseilles, *Empire colonial et capitalisme français: Histoire d'un divorce* (Paris: Albin Michel,

2005), and for his corrollary confession of neoliberal faith, see *La grande gaspillage: Les vrais comptes de l'État* (Paris: Plon, 2002).

2 Etienne Balibar, "Sujets ou citoyens? (Pour l'égalité)" *Les Temps Modernes* 40 (1984): 1742.

3 Ibid, 1743. Balibar is interested in the unjust constitutional order that immigrant workers—mostly from the former colonies—suffered in the period after decolonization and during the economic depression of the 1980s. He sees the injustice (*l'idéologie colonialiste*) originating in the era of modern republicanism, and gradually growing to the present day.

4 Ann Laura Stoler has written an important book on Foucault and empire: *Race and the Education of Desire: Foucault's History of Sexuality and the Colonial Order of Things* (Durham, NC: Duke University Press, 1995). The intellectual genealogy, in particular of Foucault's modal figure of the panopticon, is of course Jeremy Bentham and, more broadly, the philosophic radicals around him. Several of these, including the Mills, worked for the East India Company. J. S. Mill's essay *On Liberty* contains that notorious exception to the right of equal liberty for all except certain peoples still in their infancy, that is, the black, yellow, and brown parts of the British Empire.

5 Claude Liauzu, "Troubles identitaires et poids du colonial," paper presented at the annual meeting of the Society for French Historical Studies, Paris, 20 June 2004.

6 On the complex relationship between subjects and citizens in the ancien régime, see the excellent study of Peter Sahlins, *Unnaturally French: Foreign Citizens in the Old Regime and After* (Ithaca, NY: Cornell University Press, 2004); and Gail Bossenga, "Rights and Citizens in the Old Regime," *French Historical Studies* 20 (1997): 217–43.

7 See a version of Jacques Derrida's wonderful deconstruction of the slave owner Thomas Jefferson's text calling for liberty for the Americans, which appropriately Derrida first gave as a talk at the University of Virginia: Jacques Derrida, "Declaration of Independence," trans. Thomas Keenan and Thomas Pepper, *New Political Science* 15 (1986): 3–19.

8 On post-primitivism (my word), see, for example, "Africa Remix" the traveling exhibition shown June through August 2005 at the Centre Pompidou of the work of contemporary third world, but modern, sculptors, most of them living and working the West. The show has been in Germany, London, and will go to Japan next. The catalogue: Lucy Durán, David Elliott, Jean-Hubert Martin, Abdelwahab Meddeb, Simon Njami, John Picton, et al. *Africa Remix: Contemporary Art of a Continent* (London: Hayward, 2005).

SELECTED WORKS OF AMERICAN

CULTURAL HISTORY WRITING

Perry Anderson, *Considerations on Western Marxism* (London: Verso, 1976).

Joyce Appleby, Lynn Hunt, and Margaret Jacob, *Telling the Truth about History* (New York: Norton, 1995).

Judith Butler and Joan W. Scott, eds., *Feminists Theorize the Political* (New York: Routledge, 1992).

Craig Calhoun, ed., *Habermas and the Public Sphere* (Cambridge, MA, 1993).

Alex Callinicos, *Against Postmodernism: A Marxist Critique* (London: Palgrave, 1990).

Michel de Certeau, *The Practice of Everyday Life*, trans. Steven Rendell (Berkeley: University of California Press, 2002).

James Clifford, *The Predicament of Culture: Twentieth-Century Ethnography, Literature, and Art* (Cambridge, MA: Harvard University Press, 1988).

Frederick Cooper and Ann Laura Stoler, eds., *Tensions of Empire: Colonial Cultures in a Bourgeois World* (Berkeley: University of California Press, 1997).

François Cusset, *French Theory: Foucault, Derrida, Deleuze, and Cie et les mutations de la vie intellectuelle aux Etats-Unis* (Paris: La Découverte, 2003).

Robert Darnton, *The Great Cat Massacre and Other Episodes in French Cultural History* (New York: Basic Books, 1984).

——, *The Literary Underground of the Old Regime* (Cambridge, MA: Harvard University Press, 1982).

Natalie Zemon Davis, *Fiction in the Archives: Pardon Tales and Their Tellers in Sixteenth Century France* (Stanford, CA, 1987).

——, *The Return of Martin Guerre* (Cambridge, MA: Harvard University Press, 1983).

——, *Society and Culture in Early Modern France: Eight Essays* (Stanford: Stanford University Press, 1975).

Laura Lee Downs, *Writing Gender History* (London: Hodder Arnold, 2004).

Geoff Eley, "De l'histoire sociale au 'tournant linguistique' dans l'historiographie anglo-américaine des années 1980," *Genèses: Sciences Sociales et Histoire*, no. 7 (1992), 163–93.

Christian Faure, *Le projet culturel de Vichy: Folklore et révolution nationale, 1940–44* (Lyons: Presse Universitaire de Lyon, 1989).

Michel Foucault, *The Foucault Reader*, ed. Paul Rabinow (New York: Pantheon, 1984)

Clifford Geertz, *The Interpretation of Cultures: Selected Essays* (New York: Basic Books, 1973).

Eugene Genovese, *Roll, Jordon, Roll: The World the Slaves Made* (New York: Pantheon, 1974).

——, *The World the Slaveholders Made: Two Essays in Interpretation* (New York: Vintage, 1971).

Paul Gilroy, *The Black Atlantic: Modernity and Double Consciousness* (Cambridge, MA: Harvard University Press, 1993).

Carlo Ginzburg, *The Cheese and the Worms: The Cosmos of a Sixteenth-Century Miller*, trans. John Tedeschi and Anne Tedeschi (Baltimore, MD: Johns Hopkins University Press, 1980).

Harvey Goldberg, *The Life of Jean Jaurès* (Madison: University of Wisconsin Press, 1962).

Ranajit Guha, ed., *A Subaltern Studies Reader, 1986–1995* (Minneapolis: University of Minnesota Press, 1997).

Herbert Gutman, *Work, Culture, and Society in Industrializing America: Essays in American Working-Class and Social History* (New York: Viking, 1976).

Donna Haraway, *Primate Visions: Gender, Race, and Nature in the World of Modern Science* (New York: Routledge, 1985).

Carla Hesse, *The Other Enlightenment: How French Women Became Modern* (Princeton, NJ: Princeton University Press, 2003).

Eric Hobsbawm, "Perspectives on the Twentieth Century," lecture presented at the monthly Seminar on the International History of the Working at Columbia University, 18 November 1992.

Lynn Hunt, "The Paradoxical Origins of Human Rights" in *Human Rights and Revolution*, ed. Hunt et al. (London: Rowman and Littlefield, 2003), 3–18.

——, ed., *The New Cultural History* (Berkeley: University of California Press, 1989).

Noel Ignatiev, *How the Irish Became White* (New York: Routledge, 1995).

Mathew Frye Jacobson, *Whiteness of a Different Color: European Immigrants and the Alchemy of Race* (Cambridge, MA: Harvard University Press, 1998).

Patrick Joyce, "The End of Social History?" *Social History* 20 (1995): 73–91.

——, "History and Postmodernism," *Past and Present*, no. 133 (1991): 204–13.

Dominick LaCapra, *History and Criticism* (Ithaca, NY: Cornell University Press, 1985).

——, *History, Politics, and the Novel* (Ithaca, NY: Cornell University Press, 1987).

——, *Rethinking Intellectual History: Texts, Contexts, Language* (Ithaca, NY: Cornell University Press, 1983).

Joan Landes, *Women and the Public Sphere in the Age of the French Revolution* (Ithaca, NY: Cornell University Press, 1988).

Herman Lebovics, *Bringing the Empire Back Home: France in the Age of Globalization* (Durham, NC: Duke University Press, 2004).

——, *True France: The Wars over Cultural Identity* (Ithaca, NY: Cornell University Press, 1992).

——, "Post-Colonial Museums: How the French and American Models Differ," *History News Network,* http://hnn.us/articles/6939.html.

Lawrence Levine et al., "Forum on Culture," *American Historical Review* 97 (1992): 1369–430.

Patricia Mainardi, *Art and Politics of the Second Empire: The Universal Expositions of 1855 and 1867* (London and New Haven, CT: Yale University Press, 1987).

——, *The End of the Salon: Art and the State in the Early Third Republic* (Cambridge: Cambridge University Press, 1993).

Donald/Deirdre N. McCloskey, *If You're So Smart: The Narrative of Economic Expertise* (Chicago: University of Chicago Press, 1990).

——, *The Rhetoric of Economics* (Madison: University of Wisconsin Press, 1985).

Gérard Noiriel, *Le creuset français: Histoire de l'immigration, XIXe–XXe siècles* (Paris: Le Seuil, 1988).

——, *La tyrannie du national: Le droit d'asile en Europe, 1793–1993* (Paris: Calmann-Lévy, 1991).

Jeremy Popkin, "The Concept of Public Opinion in the Historiography of the French Revolution: A Critique," *Storia della Storiografia* 20 (1991): 77–92.

Anson Rabinbach, *In the Shadow of Catastrophe: German Intellectuals between Apocalypse and Enlightenment* (Berkeley: University of California Press, 1997).

Jean-Pierre Rioux, ed., *La vie culturelle sous Vichy* (Bruxelles: Complexe, 1990).

Londa Schiebinger, *The Mind Has No Sex? Women in the Origins of Modern Science* (Cambridge, MA: Harvard University Press, 1989).

Karl Schorske, *German Social Democracy, 1905–1917: The Development of the Great Schism* (1955; Cambridge, MA: Harvard University Press, 1970).

Joan W. Scott, " 'Experience,' " in *Feminists Theorize the Political,* ed. Judith Butler and Scott (New York: Routledge, 1992), 22–40.

——, *Gender and the Politics of History* (New York: Columbia University Press, 1988).

——, *The Glassworkers of Carmaux: French Craftsmen and Political Action in a Nineteenth-Century French City* (Cambridge, MA: Harvard University Press, 1974).

William Sewell, *Work and Revolution in France: The Language of Labor from the Old Regime to 1848* (Cambridge, MA: Harvard University Press, 1980).

Debora Silverman, *Art Nouveau in Fin-de-Siècle France: Politics, Psychology, and Style* (Berkeley: University of California Press, 1989).

E. P. Thompson, *Customs in Common* (London: Merlin, 1991).

——, *The Making of the English Working Class,* 1st ed. 1963 (New York: Vintage, 1966).

——, "The Moral Economy of the English Crowd in the Eighteenth Century," *Past and Present,* no. 50 (1971): 76–136.

——, "Time, Work-Discipline, and Industrial Capitalism," *Past and Present,* no. 38 (1967): 56–97.

Charles Tilly, ed., *Citizenship, Identity, and Social History* (Cambridge: Cambridge University Press, 1996).

——, *Durable Inequality* (Berkeley: University of California Press, 1998).

——, *The Rebellious Century, 1830–1930* (Cambridge, MA: Harvard University Press, 1975).

——, *As Sociology Meets History* (New York: Academic Press, 1981).

——, *Stories, Identities, and Political Change* (Lanham, MD: Rowman and Littlefield, 2002).

——, *The Vendee* (Cambridge, MA: Harvard University Press, 1964).

Hayden White, *Contents of Form: Narrative, Discourse, and Historical Representation* (Baltimore, MD: Johns Hopkins University Press, 1987).

——, *Tropics of Discourse: Essays in Cultural Criticism* (Baltimore, MD: Johns Hopkins University Press, 1978).

INDEX

Page numbers in italics refer to illustrations.

HERMAN LEBOVICS

is a Professor of History

at the State University of

New York at Stony Brook.